Native Foods of Latin America

POTATOES / PAPAS

Inés Vaughn
Traducción al español: Ma. Pilar Sanz

PowerKiDS press. & **Editorial Buenas Letras**™
New York

For Rachel who never believes that potatoes are not from Ireland
- Mauricio

Published in 2009 by The Rosen Publishing Group, Inc.
29 East 21st Street, New York, NY 10010

First Edition

Editor: Amelie von Zumbusch
Book Design: Kate Laczynski
Photo Researcher: Jessica Gerweck

Photo Credits: Cover, p. 1 © Acme Food Arts/Getty Images, Inc.; cover texture © www.istockphoto.com/ Stephen Rees; p. 4 © FhF Greenmedia/Getty Images; p. 7 © Jenny Acheson/Getty Images; pp. 8, 12 Shutterstock.com; pp. 11, 20 © Getty Images; p. 15 Wikimedia Commons; p. 16 © Jean-Léo Dugast/Peter Arnold, Inc.; p. 19 © Mike Kolloffel/Peter Arnold, Inc.

Library of Congress Cataloging-in-Publication Data

Vaughn, Inés.
  Potatoes = Papas / Inés Vaughn ; traducción al español, Ma. Pilar Sanz. — 1st ed.
    p. cm. — (Native foods of Latin America)
  Includes index.
  ISBN 978-1-4358-2728-8 (lib. binding)
  1. Cookery (Potatoes)—Juvenile literature. 2. Potatoes—Latin America—Juvenile literature. 3. Potatoes—Juvenile literature. I. Title. II. Title: Papas.
  TX803.P8V38 2009
  641.3′521098—dc22
                                                2008029354

Manufactured in the United States of America

CONTENTS

CONTENIDO

Potatoes are unlike any other crop in the world. For one thing, the part of a potato that people eat is the tuber, or the special stem that grows underground. Also, while most other plants we eat grow from seeds, potatoes grow from parts, called eyes, that dot the outside of the tuber.

Las papas son un cultivo muy especial. Para comenzar, la parte de la papa que comemos es el tubérculo, que es un tipo de raíz que crece bajo tierra. Además, mientras la mayoría de las plantas crecen de semillas, las papas crecen de una parte muy especial llamada ojos, que salen del tubérculo.

Potatoes came from South America's Andes mountains, where they grow wild. The Andes spread across Colombia, Ecuador, Peru, Bolivia, and Chile. The wild potatoes of the Andes have small, twisted tubers in many colors. There are more than 100 kinds of wild potatoes.

Las papas vienen de las montañas de los Andes, en Sudamérica. Los Andes son una cadena montañosa que atraviesa Colombia, Ecuador, Perú, Bolivia y Chile. Las papas silvestres de los Andes tienen tubérculos pequeños y retorcidos de muchos colores. Hay más de 100 clases de papas silvestres.

The first people to plant and grow potatoes were Native Americans living in the Andes. It was hard work to grow potatoes on the steep mountainsides, though. Therefore, a Native American group, called the Incas, built **terraced** fields in which to grow potatoes.

Los indígenas de los Andes fueron los primeros en cultivar papas. Cultivar papas en las empinadas montañas de los Andes era muy difícil. Es por eso que el grupo indígena conocido como los incas, construyó campos de cultivo en **terrazas** en las que cultivaban las papas.

In the 1500s, Spanish soldiers arrived in South America. They were in search of gold, and they fought and **conquered** the Incas. The Spanish carried much of the Incas' gold back to Europe with them. Along with the gold, they brought Incan crops, such as potatoes.

En el siglo 16, los soldados españoles llegaron a Sudamérica. Los españoles venían a buscar oro y pelearon y **conquistaron** a los incas. Los españoles llevaron el oro de los incas a Europa. Además del oro, los españoles llevaron cultivos incas, como las papas, a Europa.

11

Even after the arrival of the Spanish, potatoes continued to be important in the Andes. Today, more kinds of potatoes are grown in Peru than are found anywhere else in the world. Peru's potatoes come in many shapes, colors, and sizes. Peru even has purple potatoes!

Después de la llegada de los españoles, las papas siguieron siendo muy importantes en los Andes. Hoy, más clases de papas se cultivan en los Andes que en cualquier otra parte del mundo. Las papas en Perú son de todos colores, formas y tamaños. ¡En Perú hay papas hasta de color púrpura!

As you might guess, Peru is home to many wonderful potato dishes. One such dish is *papas a la Huancaína*. It is made with chiles, cheese, and potatoes. Peruvians also enjoy *causa limeña*, a special potato dish that is **layered** and cut like a cake.

Como puedes imaginar, en Perú hay muchos platillos que llevan papas. Uno de estos son las papas a la Huancaína, que llevan chiles, queso y papas. Los peruanos también disfrutan de un plato especial con papas que se llama causa limeña, en el que papas rebanadas se arreglan en capas, como un pastel.

15

Native Americans in Peru and nearby Bolivia make potatoes into *chuño*. This is a very old method of preserving potatoes. Potatoes are spread on the ground and left to **freeze** over several nights. They are then pressed into dry, light chuño. Chuño is put into soups or ground into flour.

Los indígenas de Perú y Bolivia hacen chuño con papas. Este es un método muy viejo de conservar las papas en el que se tienden en el suelo y se dejan **congelar** durante varias noches. Las papas se aplastan y secan para formar el chuño. El chuño se usa en sopas y en harinas.

Though potatoes were once eaten only in the Andes, they spread to other parts of Latin America after the coming of the Spanish. *Papas rellenas*, or fried potatoes stuffed with meat, are well liked in Cuba. In Guatemala, people eat *paches de papa*, or potato tamales.

Antiguamente, las papas sólo se comían en los Andes pero, con la llegada de los españoles, se extendieron a otras partes de Latinoamérica. En Cuba las papas rellenas, o papas fritas rellenas de carne, son muy populares. En Guatemala se comen los paches de papa, o tamales de papa.

20

Potatoes are a key food in other parts of the world, too. By the 1700s, potatoes had spread throughout Europe. In Ireland, they quickly became the chief food that people ate. Then, in the 1840s, a **blight** struck Ireland's potatoes. Many people died or moved away from Ireland forever.

Las papas han sido un alimento muy importante en otras partes del mundo. En el siglo 16, las papas se habían extendido por toda Europa. En Irlanda muy pronto se convirtieron en el alimento principal del país. Pero, en 1840, una **plaga** afectó las papas de Irlanda. Muchas personas murieron o se mudaron de Irlanda.

While potatoes played a sad part in Ireland's past, they are still loved there. In fact, this Latin American crop is loved around the world. Potatoes are very **nutritious** and can be prepared in many different ways. In 1995, they even became the first vegetable to be grown in space!

Aunque las papas tienen una triste historia en Irlanda, este cultivo sigue siendo muy querido en ese país. De hecho, las papas son muy populares en todo el mundo. Además, las papas son muy **nutritivas** y se pueden preparar de muchas maneras. ¡En 1995, las papas se convirtieron en la primera verdura cultivada en el espacio!

MINUTE
GUIDE TO
cc:Mail
with cc:Mobile

Kate Miller

A Division of Macmillan Computer Publishing

A Prentice Hall Macmillan Company

201 West 103rd Street, Indianapolis, Indiana 46290 USA

SO-ANF-875

International Standard Book Number:1-56761-587-2
Library of Congress Catalog Card Number: 94-72769

95   8   7   6   5

Interpretation of the printing code: the rightmost number of the first series
of numbers is the year of the book's printing; the rightmost number of the
second series of numbers is the number of the book's printing. For
example, a printing code of 94-1 shows that the first printing of the book
occurred in 1994.

Screen reproductions in this book were created by means of the program
Collage Plus from Inner Media, Inc., Hollis, NH.

*Special thanks to Stephen Londergan for ensuring the technical accuracy
of this book.*

Printed in the United States of America

Publisher: *Marie Butler-Knight*
Product Development Manager: *Faithe Wempen*
Managing Editor: *Elizabeth Keaffaber*
Acquisitions Manager: *Barry Pruett*
Production Editor: *Michelle Shaw*
Copy Editor: *Audra Gable*
Book Designer: *Barbara Kordesh*
Indexer:*Chris Cleveland*
Production: *Brad Chinn, Kim Cofer, Lisa Daugherty, David Dean,
Cynthia Drouin, Jennifer Eberhardt, Erika Millen, Beth Rago,
Karen Walsh, Robert Wolf*

Contents

Trademarks

All terms mentioned in this book that are known to be trademarks or service marks are listed below. In addition, terms suspected of being trademarks or service marks have been appropriately capitalized. Que cannot attest to the accuracy of this information. Use of a term in this book should not be regarded as affecting the validity of any trademark or service mark.

Microsoft Windows and Microsoft Word are trademarks of Microsoft Corporation.

Introduction

The phrase "Let's talk..." doesn't always mean verbal or paper communication anymore. A more efficient way to "talk" in many organizations is via mail of the electronic variety. cc:Mail for Windows is a top-notch vehicle for sending, receiving, and forwarding mail. In addition, cc:Mail has a host of advanced features to streamline your work.

Your New Postal Service

The workings of cc:Mail for Windows is comparable to the old, familiar postal service with a few twists. Instead of sending letters, you'll use cc:Mail to send *messages*. Messages may have attachments including other files, graphics, or FAX pages. Composing messages is a snap with cc:Mail's sophisticated text editor and spell checker.

When a message is sent to you, it is stored in your mailbox, which is called your *inbox*. Your inbox also stores receipts confirming the delivery of messages you've sent to others. Once you have read your messages, you can delete the messages or store them in *folders* or in *archive*.

To make mail routing easier, cc:Mail for Windows provides the equivalent of an address book. For example, there is a *directory* which lists all the people and post offices available for message exchange. Public and private *mailing lists*, which are shorter lists of message destinations used by you and others, can also be created. Finally, there are public places to store mail for viewing by others. These are called *bulletin boards*.

All this mail routing and storage is controlled through *post offices*, of which the cc:Mail Administrator is the postmaster general. The cc:Mail Administrator is your contact for any special mail routing problems you may encounter.

Why the 10 Minute Guide to cc:Mail with cc:Mobile?

The *10 Minute Guide to cc:Mail with cc:Mobile* is the quick and efficient route to using cc:Mail. Because each lesson is designed to be completed in 10 minutes or less, you'll be sending and receiving messages literally in a matter of minutes. In about four hours, you'll know as much about cc:Mail as you may ever need.

Although you can jump between lessons to learn only what you want to know, I recommend that you start at the beginning and work your way through. The "must learn" basic activities of sending and receiving messages are covered in early lessons. Those skills are amplified in later lessons, which cover more advanced features. Whatever you do, don't miss the front and back covers. The inside front cover tells you how to install cc:Mail on your hard disk (if the cc:Mail Administrator did not take care of that for you) and a list of the SmartIcons can be found on the inside back cover.

Conventions Used in This Book

To help you move through the lessons easily, these conventions are used:

On-screen text	On-screen text will appear in a special computer font.
What you type	Information you type will appear in a bold, color computer font.
Items you select	Commands, options, and icons you select or keys you press will appear in color.
Selection keys	Boldface letters within a menu title, menu option, or dialog box option indicate selection keys for keyboard shortcuts. These correspond to the underlined letters on-screen.

Key combinations   In many cases, you are instructed to press a two-key combination in order to enter a command. When the text says "press Alt+X," it means to hold down the Alt key while you press X. Then release both keys.

In addition to these conventions, the *10 Minute Guide to cc:Mail with cc:Mobile* uses the following icons to identify helpful information:

Plain English   New or unfamiliar terms are defined in (you got it) "plain English."

Timesaver Tips   Look here for ideas that cut corners and avoid confusion.

Panic Button   This icon identifies areas where new users often run into trouble and offers practical solutions to those problems.

For More Information

cc:Mail works with Microsoft Windows. I assume that you have a basic understanding of how to use Windows. If not, you may want to check out Appendix A for a quick overview before proceeding with cc:Mail. If you need more detailed information, the following book may be of help:

10 Minute Guide to Windows 3.1, by Kate Barnes, published by Que.

Lesson

Starting and Leaving cc:Mail

In this lesson, you will learn how to start cc:Mail, explore the cc:Mail application window, and quit cc:Mail.

Starting cc:Mail for Windows

Windows Anyone? Starting and using cc:Mail for Windows requires that you have some understanding of Microsoft Windows. Appendix A, Microsoft Windows Primer, is a quick way to learn or review the basics.

Once cc:Mail for Windows is installed, you can start it by following these steps:

1. Double click on or select the cc:Mail 2.03 icon shown in Figure 1.1.

2. In the cc:Mail Login dialog box, change your Login name and Post Office Path (assigned by the cc:Mail Administrator) if necessary. Then enter your Password and select OK.

3. Select OK in any informational dialog boxes until a cc:Mail application window, similar to the one shown in Figure 1.2, appears.

Post Office   The post office is the central storage location for cc:Mail messages.

Figure 1.1   The cc:Mail for Windows 2.03 icon.

Menu bar   Control-menu box   Title bar   Minimize box   Restore box

Figure 1.2   The cc:Mail for Windows application window.

Smarticon palette   Status bar   Contents pane   Scroll bar

Need a Jump Start?   If you are not able to start cc:Mail for Windows, try again and carefully check the information you enter. If several tries are not successful, record the problems you've noted and contact your cc:Mail Administrator.

Password Protection   Don't forget your password and always keep it confidential. Lesson 18 covers how to change your password if it is discovered by others.

The cc:Mail for Windows Application Window

The next lesson will cover how to make selections from the cc:Mail for Windows application window. For now, take a moment to get familiar with the application window itself.

- *Title bar*   Shows the application name. In Figure 1.2, the application is called cc:Mail. When you make other selections, other titles will appear.

- *Menu bar*   Identifies the menu options available to you. Each menu contains commands that allow you to perform activities.

- *SmartIcons palette*   Displays various symbols called icons. Click on an icon with the mouse as a shortcut for using menus and commands.

- *Control-menu box*   Displays commands to move, size, minimize, maximize, or restore the active window. (The active window is the window that your are currently using.) The Control-menu box can also be used to switch between windows, close the window, access the Windows Clipboard, or go to the Windows control panel.

- *Maximize and Minimize boxes*   Change the size of the window. The Maximize box is used to maximize the size of the active window to full screen. The Minimize box reduces the active window to an icon. When maximized (as shown in the figure), you can select the *Restore box* to restore the window to its previous size and location. When minimized, select the icon and then the **Restore box**.

- *Scroll bar (at the far right)*   Appears if there is more information than will fit on the window. A *scroll bar* allows you to scroll up and down lists. You can scroll through the mail you've received by using the mouse to drag the box in the scroll bar or by clicking on the up or down arrow.

> **It's Not a Pane**   A pane is simply a division of an existing window. A pane can contain information as varied as lists, command buttons, option buttons, text boxes, or drop-down lists.

- *Container and contents panes*   The two window panes are specific to the cc:Mail application. A container is a location where mail can be placed. For example, in Figure 1.2, the Inbox is one container, while Folders, Bulletin Boards, and Archives are others. The contents pane contains a list of the items contained in the open pane. In the figure, messages stored in the Inbox are in the contents pane.

Press F6 to switch between the container pane and the contents pane. A dotted line around the selection in the pane indicates which pane is active.

The container pane and the contents pane can be sized. Using the mouse, point to the dividing line between the panes and drag the line to the desired location. Figure 1.3 shows the panes resized to show more of the container pane.

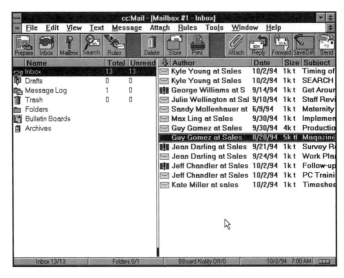

Figure 1.3   Panes resized on the cc:Mail application window.

- *Status bar (on the bottom of the screen)*   Identifies
  the number of read and unread messages in your
  inbox, folders, and bulletin boards. For example,
  Inbox 8/12 means there are 8 unread messages and
  12 total messages. The status bar also indicates the
  current date and time.

Quitting cc:Mail for Windows

There are several ways to leave cc:Mail. Use any one of the
following methods:

- Press Alt+F4 (hold down the Alt key while pressing
  the F4 key).

- Select the Exit command from the File menu. (To
  make a menu selection with the keyboard in cc:Mail,
  press Alt to go to the menu bar. Then press F for the
  File menu. Press X to Exit.)

- With the mouse, double-click the Control-menu box in the upper left corner of the cc:Mail application window.

- Click on Close from the Control menu. (To open the Control menu, click once on the Control-menu box or press Alt+Spacebar. Then select the Close command by pressing C.)

When you receive a message such as Exit cc:Mail?, respond by selecting Yes. You are then returned to Windows.

In this lesson, you learned how to start and quit cc:Mail for Windows and gained familiarity with the cc:Mail application window. In the next lesson, you'll learn how to make selections from the cc:Mail application window and to get help.

2

Basic cc:Mail Skills

In this lesson, you will learn how to make selections in cc:Mail, use lists, and ask for help.

Using Menus and Selecting Commands

You can use the mouse or keyboard to make menu selections. You navigate cc:Mail for Windows like any Windows application. See Appendix A for details.

SmartIcons

An alternative to using menus and commands in cc:Mail is the SmartIcon palette shown in Figure 2.1. SmartIcons are buttons that may be selected to execute commands or key presses. For example, the first SmartIcon on the left in the default SmartIcon palette may be selected to prepare a new message. The action is the equivalent of pressing Ctrl+M or selecting Message New Message. To use a SmartIcon, you must use the mouse; the keyboard will not work. To see a description of a SmartIcon, point at the icon and hold down the right mouse button. The description appears in the title bar. Release the button when you have read the description.

> **Check Out SmartIcons** Take some time to check out the SmartIcons and refer to the back cover of this book for the most often used SmartIcons. When you see a menu selection in this book, there may be a SmartIcon shortcut available. If you have used any Lotus product, such as 1-2-3, you will see the SmartIcons are very similar and work the same way.

Description

Figure 2.1   The SmartIcon palette.

Selecting from a List

Sometimes you will need to make selections from a cc:Mail
for Windows list. For example, you may want to select
several messages to move to the Trash container to be
deleted. Or you may want to select several messages to copy
to another container. Use these methods to make the selection or selections you need.

Display container items   Mouse: Double click on
                            the container.
                            Keyboard: Press the
                            arrows to highlight the
                            container and press
                            Enter.

Select item in list   Mouse: Click on the
                            item.
                            Keyboard: Press an arrow
                            key to highlight.

Select consecutive items	Mouse: Click on the first item; hold down Shift and click on the last item. Keyboard: Highlight the first item; hold down Shift and use the arrow key to move to the last item.
Select non-consecutive items	Mouse: Click on the first item; hold down Ctrl and click on each additional item. Keyboard: Highlight the first item and press and hold down Ctrl; use the arrow keys to identify the next item; press the Spacebar to select; release Ctrl when done.
Deselect all items	Release Shift or Ctrl and select another item.

Message and Container Icons

Messages and containers are designated by icons. The appearance of each icon gives you a clue as to the contents or status of the message or container. Messages sent to you that have not been opened (not yet read) appear with a closed envelope icon. Those sent to you that have been opened (read) appear with an opened envelope icon.

Containers use other icons. Table 2.1 identifies each container when it is opened (selected) and closed (deselected).

Table 2.1 Open and closed container icons.

	Open	Closed
Inbox		
Drafts		
Message Log		
Trash		
Folders container		
Individual Folder		
Bulletin Boards container		
Individual Bulletin Board		
Archives container		
Individual Archive		

Copy or Move from a List to Another Container (Including Trash)

You may want to copy or move items in a list. For example, when you finish a project, you may want to move all messages stored in the project folder to archive storage. Or you may want to move a message to the trash container to delete it.

To move or copy, you can use the mouse "drag and drop" approach described here:

1. Make sure you can locate the destination container for the selected item(s).

2. Select one or more items to copy or move.

3. To move, hold the left mouse button down and drag one of the selected icons to the destination container. (To copy, perform the same operation except also hold down the Ctrl key.)

4. Release the mouse button on the container icon.

Funny Looking Icons If the icon changes to a circle with a line through it (shown in Figure 2.2), you cannot copy or move the item to the container. If an envelope icon appears, you can complete the copy or move. The only exception is that when you send an item to the trash container, a trash can icon appears.

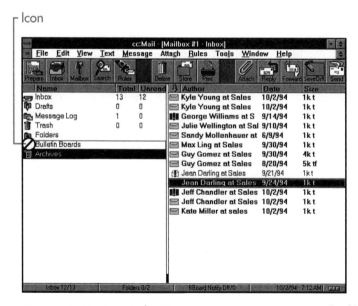

Figure 2.2 Icon indicating you cannot copy or move the file to the destination.

Instead of using the mouse, you can use the Edit menu to copy or move from one container to another. Follow these steps:

1. Make sure you can locate the container to which you want to copy or move text.

2. Select the item(s) to copy or move.

3. To copy, choose Copy from the Edit menu (or press Ctrl+C). To move, choose Cut from the Edit menu (or press Ctrl+X).

4. Select the destination container.

5. Paste the item(s) by choosing Paste from the Edit menu (or by pressing Ctrl+V).

Refreshing a List

Lists that you are using are not updated automatically during use. For example, if you are looking at the list of messages in your inbox and a new message comes in, you will need to refresh the list to make the new message appear.

To refresh a list, double-click on the icon of the open container. Or with the cursor in the list of items, press the Home or End key.

Changing the Order of a List

Messages are listed in order by date. If the arrow above the message icon column points down, the messages are ordered from the oldest to the newest. If the arrow points up, messages are listed from the most recent to the oldest. If you have a mouse, you can change the order by double clicking on the arrow until it points in the desired direction. (There is no keyboard method to change the order of the list display.)

Asking for Help

You'll be happy to know that cc:Mail for Windows has a useful help system just a keypress away. Press F1 (or select Index from the Help menu) to access the Help system index. The Help system Index is shown in Figure 2.3.

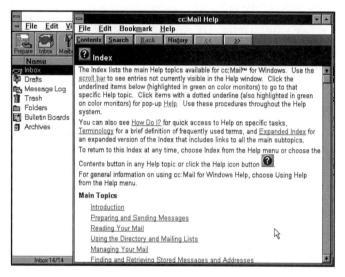

Figure 2.3   The cc:Mail Help system Index.

Click on the topic to view. Or press Tab to select the topic and then press Enter. To leave the Help system, select Exit from the File menu or double-click the Control-menu box.

While using Help, buttons are available to help you find what you need. Select the Contents button to return to the Index at any time. The Back button takes you back one help screen at a time. The History button shows the Windows Help History dialog box. Here, the screens you've accessed are listed, and the current screen is highlighted. You may select any screen.

Select the Search button, and the Search dialog box appears. To go to a new topic, just type it in, or select a topic from the list. Then, select Show Topics. The topics appear at the bottom of the window with the one closest to your entry highlighted. Make sure the topic you want is highlighted in the lower box, and then choose the Go To button. You will be taken directly to the topic.

While using Help, pay special attention to the words and phrases in green. Those with a solid underline can be selected to go to that topic. When those underlined with a dotted line are selected, a definition appears. To select, click on the word or phrase or use the Tab key to highlight the word or phrase, and then press Enter.

In this lesson, you learned how to make selections and use lists as well as get help. In the next lesson, you will learn how to create and send a simple message.

Lesson

3

Creating and Sending a Message

In this lesson, you will learn how to prepare a message to be sent and how to send the message.

Creating and Sending a New Message

When you select New Message from the Message menu, the Message Window appears. Figure 3.1 shows the elements of this window. Use the Address button to select addresses. In the *address mode list*, you can select from TO to identify the addressee of the message, CC to identify carbon copy recipients, and BCC to identify blind carbon copy recipients.

> **Copy Me**   Carbon copy recipients are known to all recipients. Blind carbon copy recipients are not revealed to other message recipients, including other blind carbon copy recipients.

In the *address text box,* you can enter the name of a recipient (last name first). As you type, cc:Mail for Windows checks the Directory and enters the name for you. If the name that appears isn't quite right, use the arrow keys to scroll through the names in the Directory. Stop when you have the desired name.

On the Message Window, you can enter any *special handling instructions* (covered in Lesson 9). If attachments are added to the message, they appear in the *list of attachments* area. (Attachments are discussed in Lesson 10.) In the *subject text box*, enter the subject of the message. (Or, if subjects have been entered, you can select them by choosing the Subject button.) Finally, the *item-view pane* is where the body of the message is entered.

> **Adding Subjects** You can add a subject you've entered to the subject list, which is a handy storage place for commonly used subjects such as "Weekly Status Report" or "Management Meeting Minutes." To add a subject to the list, select the **S**ubject button and enter the subject. Then select **A**dd to List and Cancel.

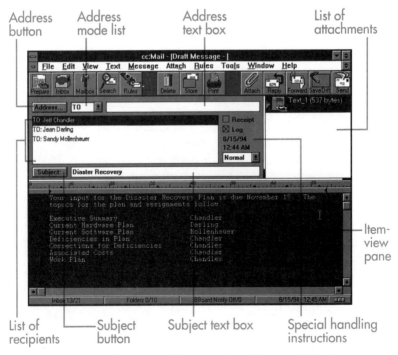

Figure 3.1 The cc:Mail for Windows Message Window.

To create and send a new message, follow these steps.

1. Select New Message from the Message menu. The Message Window appears.

2. In the address mode list, select the type of mode. Press Tab to move to the Address text box or click on the Address text box.

3. With the cursor in the Address text box, type in the last name and then first name of the person. Press Enter to add the name to the list of recipients.

4. Repeat steps 2 and 3 until all recipients are added. Press Enter to go to the Subject text box or click on the Subject text box.

5. Enter the subject, or choose the Subject button and select a previously stored subject. Press Enter or click in the item-view pane.

6. Enter the mail message in the item-view pane.

7. Select Send from the Message menu or press Ctrl+S to send the mail to all of the recipients.

Saving a Draft

Occasionally, you may want to work on a draft of a message, save it, and then return later to complete and send the message. To defer sending the message, select Save Draft from the Message menu. The message is saved in the Drafts container. To complete the draft later, select the Drafts container and then choose the message to complete.

Selecting from the Address Message Dialog Box

What if you can't remember the name of the recipient? You can use the Address Message dialog box to select a name.

Instead of typing in a name, select the Address button or choose Address from the Message menu. The Address Message dialog box shown in Figure 3.2 appears.

Address mode list   Address text box

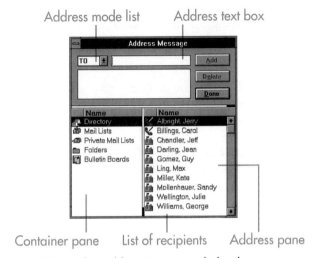

Container pane   List of recipients   Address pane

Figure 3.2 The Address Message dialog box.

This dialog box has an address mode list, Address text box, and list of recipients like the Message Window. In addition, it has a *container pane* and *address pane*. Open the container to access the addresses from which you want to select. In the figure, the Directory container is open. Double-click on the name you want or highlight it using your arrow keys and select Add. The name is placed in the list of recipients.

Drag and Drop You can also use the drag and drop procedure described in the last lesson to enter one or more names in the list of recipients.

Finding Names Fast The names that appear in the address pane may be numerous. Use the scroll bar or type in the first few letters of the last name in the address text box to move to a name with those letters. Use the arrow keys to refine the selection from there.

If you accidentally enter a name (or enter it with the wrong address mode), highlight the name in the list of recipients and select the Delete button or press Del.

When all recipients are entered, select Done. The names appear in the list of recipients in the Message Window.

Using the Address Book

Choosing the recipients from the Address Book is an alternative to selecting names from the Address Message dialog box. Follow these steps to use the Address Book:

1. From the Message Window, select New Address Book Window from the Window menu. The Address Book Mail List dialog box (shown as the top window in Figure 3.3) appears.

2. Open the desired address book (the mailbox icon appears open).

3. Select one or more names using any of the selection methods described for the Address Message dialog box, including drag and drop. (Figure 3.3 shows the icon that appears when one or more selected names are dragged to the list of recipients.)

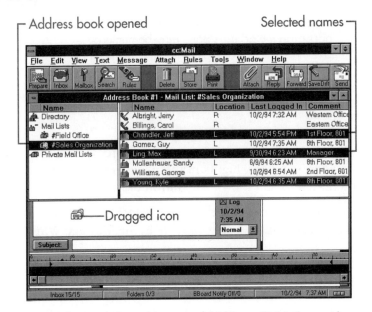

Figure 3.3 The Address Book Mail List dialog box with selections made and the icon dragged to the Message Window list of recipients.

I Lost My Window When you select New Address **B**ook from the **W**indow menu, the Address Book Mail List dialog box may take up the whole screen. To see both the dialog box and the Message Window, select **T**ile Vertical or Tile **H**orizontal from the **W**indow menu.

In this lesson, you learned how to prepare and send a simple message. In the next lesson, you'll learn how to edit a message.

Lesson

Editing Text in cc:Mail Messages

In this lesson, you will learn how to select text, delete text, add text from a file, control the appearance of text, and set margins and tabs.

Moving the Cursor and Selecting Text

You will use the keyboard to make quick cursor movements in a message. Pressing the Shift key at the same time as any of the cursor movement keys listed below selects (highlights) text to be manipulated further. Table 4.1 shows the most common cursor movement keypresses.

Table 4.1 Cursor movement keys.

Press	To move the cursor to . . .
Arrow	New location
Home	Beginning of line
End	End of line
PgUp	Up one window
PgDn	Down one window
Ctrl+Home	Beginning of document
Ctrl+End	End of document

Deselect Please Once text is selected, you can deselect it simply by moving the cursor or clicking the mouse.

Deleting Text

To delete text to the right of the cursor, press the Del key. To delete text to the left of the cursor, press the Backspace key. Pressing Ctrl+Del deletes to the end of the line. Another alternative is to select text using Shift and one of the cursor movement keypresses in Table 4.1 to select the text and then press Del.

Inserting Text from a File

Rather than type in all your text in a message, you may want to enter text in a file and then bring it into a message. This feature is useful if you are sending a paper memo to some people and a cc:Mail for Windows message to others. Or you may want to include text from an existing report or letter in a message without having to reenter the text.

To insert text from a file, follow these steps:

1. Position the cursor in the message where the text is to appear.

2. Select Import from the File menu.

3. From the Import dialog box, select the drive, path, and file to import.

4. When the file name appears in the File Name text box, select OK. The text from the file is placed in the message.

Controlling the Appearance of Text

You can control the font, style, and size of text in a message. These features are handy to affect the appearance of your message.

Font, Style, and Size? The font is the type of text such as Courier. Only monospaced fonts (where each character is the same width) can be used. The style includes options like italic and bold. The size is expressed numerically in points.

These are the steps to change the font, style, and size of text in a message:

1. Choose Fonts from the Text menu.

2. In the User Setup dialog box, choose Select Font to identify what the font affects. Then select Change Font.

3. The Font dialog box appears (see Figure 4.1). Select a Font, Font Style, and Size. The text Sample shows the appearance of the text you've selected.

4. Select OK.

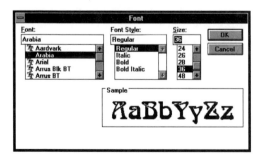

Figure 4.1 The Font dialog box.

Using Color to Emphasize

Color can emphasize text in your messages. By setting the
pen color, you can control the color of the foreground text
characters, as well as that of the background on which they
appear. You can also set the *page color*, which is the color of
the item-view pane. If no page color is set, the background
pen color can be used.

To change the pen color, follow these steps:

1. Select the text to highlight.

2. Press the right mouse button or select Colors from
   the Text menu (or press Ctrl+H). The Color Highlighting dialog box appears (see Figure 4.2).

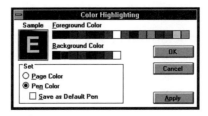

Figure 4.2 The Color Highlighting dialog box.

3. Select the Pen Color option button. Select the
   Foreground Color and then Background Color until
   the Sample shows the correct color combination. (A
   green line appears around each color selection.)

4. To apply the pen color to the message text, choose
   Apply.

5. Check the message's appearance. If you are satisfied
   with the way it looks, select OK.

To set the page color, follow these steps:

1. Make sure the cursor is in the item-view pane and positioned where the new page color is to begin.

2. Press the right mouse button or select Colors from the Text menu (or press Ctrl+H). The Color Highlighting dialog box appears.

3. Select the Page Color option. Select the Background color.

4. When the sample is appropriate, select OK.

Setting Margins and Tabs

You can change the margins and tab settings in a message to fit your needs. Regardless of the font size you use, you can have up to 80 columns (characters) in a message line. You set the margins by specifying the number of columns from the left edge of the message. To set margins and/or tabs:

1. Select Margins/Tabs from the Text menu.

2. In the Margins/Tabs dialog box, enter the column number that you want to designate as the Left and Right margins. (To make the settings the new default, select Save.)

3. To change the number of columns between tab stops, enter the number for Tab Stops.

4. Select OK.

Another way to control margins is to use the Ruler. If the Ruler does not appear, choose Ruler from the Text menu to see the Ruler (shown in Figure 4.3). Using the mouse, drag the margin markers to where you want the margins. As you can see in the figure, tab markers also appear on the Ruler. However, you cannot change tabs from the Ruler. Use the Margins/Tab dialog box to change tabs.

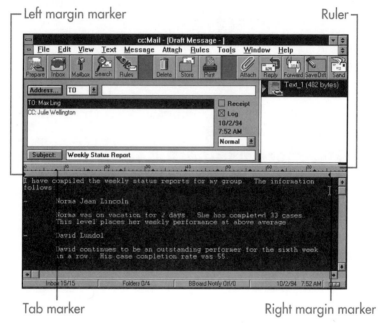

Figure 4.3 The Ruler.

In this lesson, you learned how to edit a message by selecting and deleting text, inserting file text, changing the look of the message, and setting margins and tabs. In the next lesson, you will learn advanced editing features, such as undoing mistakes, copying and moving text, and finding and replacing text.

Lesson

Advanced Editing

In this lesson, you will learn how to undo edits, copy and move text, and find and replace text.

Using Undo

Whoops! Everyone can make a mistake. When you do, undo right away. For example, if you just accidentally deleted some text, undo, and the text is returned to the message. To undo, just select Undo from the Edit menu or press Ctrl+Z. Your last edit is restored.

> **THAT'S Not What I Meant To Do!** You must use Undo immediately after the action you want to undo. cc:Mail will always undo the last action taken, so be careful not to continue working and then try to go back and undo an action that you had previously made. The Undo feature only remembers one action at a time and you may end up undoing something that you didn't intend to undo.

Cut, Copy, and Paste

To make creating messages easier, you can copy or move text.

Cut, Copy, and Paste   When you move text, you *cut* it out of the current location (the text is removed). Then you *paste* it into the new location. When you copy text, you *copy* it from the current location (the original version stays in place). Then you paste the text into a new location. The most recent cut or copy is stored in the Clipboard, which is a temporary storage location.

Plain English

To copy or move text, follow these steps:

1. Select the text to copy or move.

2. Select Cut (or press Ctrl+X) or Copy (or press Ctrl+C).

3. Move the cursor to the new location and select Paste (or press Ctrl+V).

Figure 5.1 shows the text Weekly Status Report after it was copied from the Subject text box to the item-view pane. Text can also be copied or moved within the item-view pane or between messages.

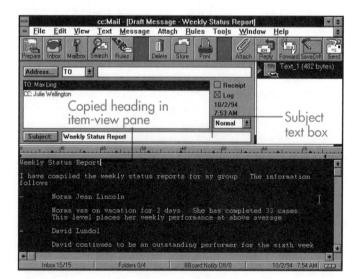

Figure 5.1 The copied heading.

Move and Copy Between Messages   To cut and copy text between messages, cut or copy the desired text. Before pasting, switch to the new message using any of the Windows approaches (see Appendix A). Then paste the text.

Paste Again   When you cut or copy text, the text is placed in the Clipboard, where it remains until new text is cut or copied. As a result, you can paste the text more than once.

Find and Replace

At some time, you might need to find specific text in large messages. Or you may need to find some specific passage and replace it with new text. The Find and Replace feature can come in handy when you need to locate that particular text string in a long message or to replace a proper name that you may have misspelled throughout your message. When you use this feature, you will be able to specify what text you want cc:Mail to find by selecting from these options:

- *Match Whole Words Only*   Finds occurrences of words as whole words only and not portions of larger words. For example, this will find "out" as a whole word but not find the word "outstanding." If you do not select this option, "outstanding" will be found when "out" is entered.

- *Match Case*   Matches the upper- and lowercase letters exactly as entered. For example, if you enter "Highway," cc:Mail will find "Highway" but not "highway."

To find text, follow these steps:

1. Put the cursor where you want the search to start.

2. Select Find/Replace from the Edit menu. The
   Replace dialog box shown in Figure 5.2 appears.

Figure 5.2 The Replace dialog box.

3. Enter the text to find in the Find What text box.
   Check Match Whole Word Only and/or Match Case
   if desired.

4. To find the next occurrence of (but not replace) the
   specified text, select Find Next.

Use F3   Once you have entered the text to find
in the Replace dialog box, you can leave the
dialog box and still find the text. Just press F3.
The text you last searched for will be located.

To find and replace text, follow these steps:

1. Put the cursor where you want the search to start.

2. Select Find/Replace from the Edit menu. The
   Replace dialog box appears.

3. Enter the text to find in the Find What text box.

4. In the Replace With text box, enter the text with which you want to replace the found text. Check Match Whole Word Only and/or Match Case if desired.

5. Select Replace if you want to confirm each replacement or select Replace All to replace every occurrence without stopping for your input.

When you select Replace in order to confirm each replacement, the first occurrence of specified text is identified. You then select Replace to replace the text and continue to the next occurrence. Or you can select Find Next to keep that occurrence as is and look for the next occurrence. In Figure 5.3, the first occurrence of "case" has been replaced with "folder." The next occurrence is now marked.

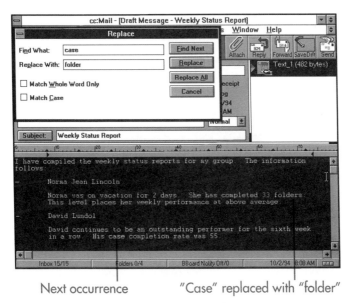

Next occurrence   "Case" replaced with "folder"

Figure 5.3 "Case" replaced with "folder."

Undo a Replacement   If you replace text using the Find/Replace command and then realize that you shouldn't have replaced it, you can undo the replacement. Select Undo from the Edit menu or press Ctrl+Z before performing any other operation.

In this lesson, you learned how to undo your work, and cut, copy, and paste text, as well as how to find and replace text. In the next lesson, you'll learn how to spell check your messages.

Lesson

Spell Checking

In this lesson, you will learn to use the spell checker and to control repeated words.

Using the Spell Checker

The cc:Mail for Windows spell checker can be used to check all or part of a message for spelling errors. When you spell check, words that do not appear in cc:Mail's dictionary are identified as misspelled. Words that appear twice in a row (for example, the the) are also identified.

The cc:Mail for Windows spell checker allows you to add words to your own personal dictionary. For example, commonly used proper names (like your own name) are good candidates to add to your personal dictionary. Professional jargon or acronyms you use often are also appropriate. Once you add a word to your personal dictionary, it is no longer identified as a misspelled word.

> **But I Spell Checked It!** Spell checking only identifies words not in the cc:Mail dictionary. It does not identify incorrect usage of words (such as two in place of to) and is no substitute for careful proofreading.

To run the spell checker, follow these steps:

1. Place the cursor where you want to begin spell checking or select the text to check. To check the entire message, place the cursor under the first character in the message.

2. From the Tools menu, select Spell Check. The Spelling dialog box appears (see Figure 6.1).

3. To replace the word, select an alternative from the Alternatives box or enter a new word in the Replace with text box, and then choose one of the replace buttons. If you don't want to replace the word, select another button. All of the buttons are described below:

Replace All	Replaces each occurrence of the word with the text you've entered in the Replace with text box.
Replace	Replaces only this single occurrence of the word with the text in the Replace with text box.
Skip All	Ignores every occurrence of the word.
Skip	Ignores only this occurrence of the word; the next occurrence will be identified.

Add to Dictionary   Adds the word to your
personal dictionary so that
it is not identified as a
misspelling in the future.

4. Continue the spell check operation until cc:Mail
indicates that the operation is complete.

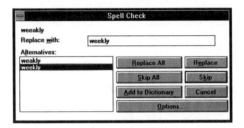

Figure 6.1 The Spelling dialog box.

Item-View Pane Only When you spell
check, the text is checked in the item-view pane
only. You will have to correct any errors in the
Subject text box yourself.

Controlling Repeated Words

If a word is repeated in a message, the spell checker displays
the dialog box shown in Figure 6.2. To remove the repeated
word and move on, select OK. The second occurrence of the
word is highlighted, and the Spelling dialog box appears.
Press Del to remove the word from the Replace with text
box and select the Replace button.

First occurrence ———   Second occurrence

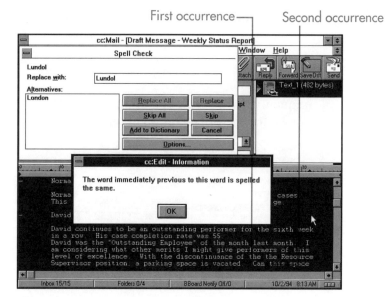

Figure 6.2 A repeated word.

Repeated Word Gone; Space Remaining   Sometimes when you remove a repeated word, an extra space or two remains. For safety, note where the repeated word appeared and check the location once the spell check is done.

In this lesson, you learned how to spell check a message. In the next lesson, you will learn how to read mail that others have composed and sent to you.

Reading Your Mail

In this lesson, you will learn how to open mail to read the contents.

The Mailbox Window

Messages may arrive in your inbox, in folders, or in a bulletin board. To see the messages in any of these containers, simply select the container. The messages are displayed in the item pane.

Finding Unread Messages

When you start cc:Mail, the cc:Mail for Windows - Notify box appears, as shown in Figure 7.1, identifying the number of unread messages. (This feature may be turned off in the user setup options. See Lesson 18 for more information.)

When viewing a list of messages, unread messages appear with a sealed envelope icon. Messages that have been read have an opened envelope icon. Take a look at Figure 7.2 where the inbox contains both unread and read messages. Some envelope icons have an exclamation point, which means the message was sent with urgent priority. Others have a downward pointing arrow indicating low priority. (Priorities are covered in Lesson 9.)

Figure 7.1 The cc:Mail for Windows - Notify dialog box indicating the number of unread messages.

Urgent priority

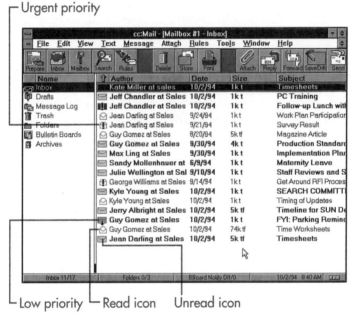

Low priority — Read icon   Unread icon

Figure 7.2 Read and unread message icons.

Read, But Understood? When a message is marked as read, it means the message has been opened in cc:Mail for Windows. It does not guarantee that the recipient actually read the message.

Reading a Message

To read your messages, the mailbox (shown in Figure 7.2) must be available. Most cc:Mail setups automatically open the mailbox when cc:Mail is started up. If yours does not, choose New Mail Box Window from the Window menu or click on the Mailbox SmartIcon. New messages appear in the Inbox. Other containers hold messages you have copied or moved to the containers. The one exception is the Bulletin Board container, which holds messages from many users. To search for specific messages, see Lessons 15 and 16. Once the mailbox appears, follow these steps to read a message:

1. Select the container holding the messages you want to read. The messages appear in the item pane.

2. Double-click on a message with the mouse, or select the message and press Enter. (You can select a read or unread message.)

3. The message is displayed in the Message Window shown in Figure 7.3.

4. Once the message is read, you can close it by pressing Ctrl+F4. Alternatively, click on or select the control-menu box for the message by pressing Alt+- (hyphen). Then select Close.

> **Go Direct**   You will often want to review several consecutive messages. Rather than open and close each message, skip directly to the previous or next message. From a message, select Next message or Previous message from the Message menu.

I Can't See!   You may want to adjust the
Message Window for easier reading. Point at the
adjustable pane separator to move the window.
The mouse pointer becomes a two-headed arrow.
Drag the separator to the desired location.

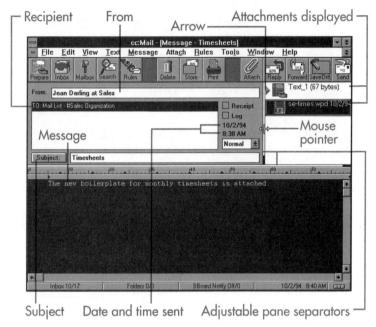

Figure 7.3 The Message Window.

Deleting Messages

To delete a message once it is read, select Delete from the
Message menu. A delete confirmation window appears.
Select OK. You can also delete messages from the list in the
mailbox item pane. Just select the message, and press or drag
the message to the trash container. A confirmation window
appears. Select OK.

Reading Attachments

Messages may have attachments (refer to Figure 7.3). An arrow in front of an attachment indicates that the contents of that attachment are displayed. In Figure 7.3, there is a file attachment called se-times. Because there is no arrow before this icon, special steps are necessary to view the contents of the attachment.

If the attachment is a file, graphic, or FAX and is a commonly used file format, use these steps to read the attachment:

1. Double-click on the attachment icon. Or select the attachment, then choose View item from the Message menu.

2. The file is displayed in the message. (If a message appears saying that there is no application associated with the item, try the following steps. If an icon appears in the message, double-click that icon.)

3. When you close the message with Ctrl+F4, the original message contents are restored.

Sometimes, you may need to run the attachment application from cc:Mail for Windows in order to view the contents. For example, if you received a spreadsheet which was created in Microsoft Excel, you might need to run Excel. To do this, the application must be available to your computer. Follow these steps to run an attachment application:

1. Hold down Shift and double-click on the attachment. Or select the attachment and choose Run Item from the Message menu. (If an alert message appears, try double-clicking without pressing Shift.)

2. The application begins and you can use it to view the attachment.

3.   To return to cc:Mail, select Exit from the File menu.

> **Editing Attachments**   If you want to edit the
> attachment, run it from the application. Make
> changes using the application and save the file
> using the File Save As command. A file is created
> that is separate from the one attached. If you use the
> File Save command to save the file, you'll be taken to
> the cc:Mail Forward/Reply dialog box to make a
> forwarding or reply selection. Lessons 11 and 12 cover
> forwarding and replying in more detail.

Other Attachment Uses

An attachment can be dragged and dropped to the attachments pane of another message. Do this if you want to include the attachment in your own original message.

What if you want to save an attachment but not the message? If you can look at an attachment, you can save it separately from the message. This way, you can delete the message but still have the attachment. To save an attachment to disk, select the attachment. From the File menu, select Save (to let cc:Mail assign a name) or Save As (to assign the name yourself). Follow the prompts. Once the attachment is saved, you may delete the message.

In this lesson, you learned how to read your mail and how to handle attachments. In the next lesson, you will learn how to print a message.

Lesson

Printing a Message

In this lesson, you will learn how to print a message or an attachment to a message.

Printing One or More Messages

Trees can breathe easier with cc:Mail for Windows in the world, because cc:Mail is designed to reduce the amount of paper passed around. However, you may occasionally want a paper copy of a message. After all, it is easier to carry a piece of paper to a meeting than it is to carry the typical workstation.

You can start the print operation from the Mailbox or a Message Window. From the Mailbox, you can select one or more messages to print. (Or select no messages to print them all.) If you start the print from the Message Window, you may only print that message.

To print one or more messages, follow these steps:

1. Select Print from the File menu (or click the Print SmartIcon).

2. The Print Options dialog box appears (see Figure 8.1). Select the item(s) to print. From an open message, select the open item, all items in the item pane, or only those items selected. From the Mailbox, select the list, all items, or specific items (text, file, or fax).

3. Select OK.

When you select OK, the Printing dialog box appears to identify how much of the print is complete. Once that dialog box goes away, you can continue your work.

Figure 8.1 The Print Options dialog box.

Controlling the Setup

You can control the printer settings by selecting the Setup button from the Print Options dialog box when you are preparing to print. Or you can select Print Setup from the File menu to enter settings outside of a print operation. In either case, the Print Setup dialog box shown in Figure 8.2 appears.

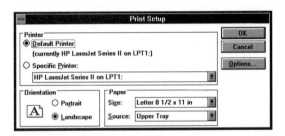

Figure 8.2 The Print Setup dialog box.

In the Print Setup dialog box, identify the printer to use. You can select the Default Printer or choose a Specific Printer from the drop-down list. Next you identify the page orientation as Portrait (the short edge at the top) or Landscape (the long edge at the top). Finally, describe the paper Size and Source location from the drop-down lists.

For other print settings specific to your printer, choose the Options button. For example, you may be able to control dithering (the fineness of the print) or the intensity of the print from dark to light.

When all printer setup alternatives are complete, select OK.

Controlling Fonts   Lesson 4 discussed how to change fonts in a message. You can also control fonts during printing. Choose the Fonts button from the Print Options dialog box to control the font used for printing. See Lesson 4 for more information about the use and availability of fonts.

Printing Attachments

In the last lesson, you learned that messages may have attachments. To print an attachment, select the attachments to print from the Message Window. Then select File Print and continue as you would with any print operation.

Can't Print the Attachment?   When printing an attachment, a dialog box may appear in which you need to select the format. Typically, printing in a DOS text or text format will get results. If you still cannot print, select the attachment and choose File Save As. Once the file is saved under a new name, print the file with the application used to create the file.

In this lesson, you learned how to control print options and print a message (including attachments). In the next lesson, you will learn how to use special handling instructions to speed delivery of messages, make copies for your log, and get a receipt when a message is read.

Lesson

Special Handling

In this lesson, you will learn how to set the delivery priority for a message, request a receipt, and send a copy to your personal log.

Special Handling Instructions

When you create a message using the New Message from the Message menu, the special handling instructions appear in the Message Window. You use the special handling instructions to request a receipt for any message you send, send a copy of a message to your personal log for future reference, and set the delivery priority for your message. Figure 9.1 shows the special handling instructions.

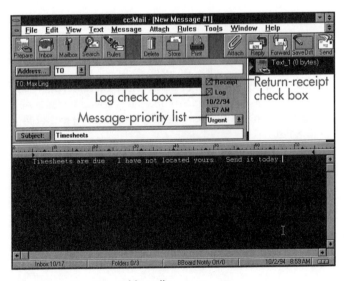

Figure 9.1   Special handling instructions.

Receipt Requested

Have you ever sent or received certified mail? If you have, you know that a receipt is returned when the mail is delivered. In cc:Mail for Windows, use the return-receipt check box to get a receipt when the primary recipients read the message.

Primary Recipients   Primary recipients include all individuals named after TO. You will not receive a receipt for CC or BCC recipients. Likewise, you will not receive a receipt if you send the message to a bulletin board or folder.

To get a receipt, check the Receipt check box on the Message Window. Click on the check box with the mouse, or use the Tab key to move to the check box and press the Spacebar.

To cancel the request for a return receipt, deselect the Receipt check box before leaving the Message Window. Otherwise, once the message is sent, the receipt is returned.

A receipt appears as a regular message in the sender's inbox. The recipient is identified as the Author. The Subject is something like Receipt of 5/5/93 8:06AM message.

Sending a Copy to Your Personal Log

You can easily save a copy of a message to refer to later. The easiest way to save a copy is to send a copy to a special cc:Mail for Windows folder called the Message Log. The Message Log is in the container pane and is shown in Figure 9.2.

Message Log

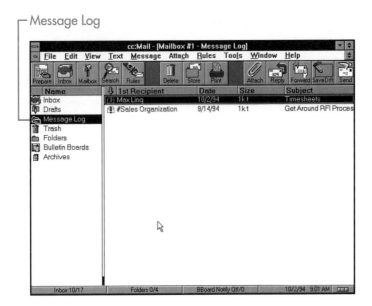

Figure 9.2 The Message Log.

I Don't Have a Message Log Don't worry if your Message Log does not appear initially. It is created the first time you log a message. (However, if the Log option is dimmed on the Message Window, the feature may not be enabled for your post office.)

To send a message to your Message Log, check the Log check box on the Message Window. To view a message in your Message Log, select the Message Log from the container pane. The messages appear. Handle the message as you would any other cc:Mail message.

Lost Message Log Messages? View your Message Log as a temporary storage location. cc:Mail for Windows can be set up to periodically clear your Message Log. To save messages permanently, place them in a folder or in archive (see Lesson 14).

Setting Message Priority

You can set a priority for each message sent. The default is Normal. Other options are Low and Urgent. Figure 9.3 shows the icons that appear for each priority setting when a message is received. (On some networks, urgent messages receive the highest routing priority.)

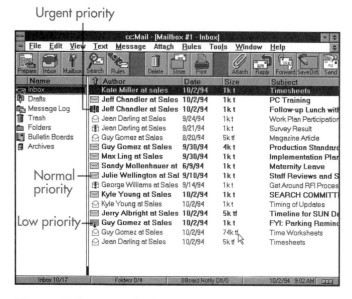

Figure 9.3 Icons which your message recipient sees.

The priority for a message is sent when the message is composed. Follow these steps:

1. From the Message Window, click on the drop-down Message-priority list (refer to Figure 9.1). Or press Tab until the Message-priority list is highlighted.

2. Designate the priority for the message by clicking on the selection with the mouse or pressing the up or down arrow key.

3. Press Tab to continue or click on another part of the Message Window.

In this lesson, you learned how to add special handling instructions to your messages. In the next lesson, you will learn how to attach items to a message.

Lesson

Adding Attachments to a Message

In this lesson, you will learn how to add attachments, such as text or files, to a message.

Attachments

> **Attachment**   Any text, file, or Fax item attached to a cc:Mail message is called an attachment.

A cc:Mail for Windows message can include up to 20 attachments, including text or graphics files and Clipboard or FAX items. You can attach an existing item to a message or create a new item that you want to attach to a message. If you create an attachment to add text to a message (instead of typing the text into the message), the attachment can easily be separated from the message and used for other purposes. (See Lesson 7 for how to read and save attachments that have been sent to you. See Lesson 8 for how to print an attachment.)

Attaching Text Items

You may attach a text item to a message. A text item is made up of text only and is created using the cc:Mail text editor. Why attach a text item to a message rather than just include the text in the message itself? Creating a text item attachment keeps the text item separate from the message. That way, the text item may be saved as a separate file or copied to other messages easily.

To attach a text item while preparing a message, follow these steps:

1. From the Message Window for a new message, open the Attach menu and select Text.

2. A new text icon appears in the attachments pane (see Figure 10.1). The arrow indicates that the attachment will contain whatever is entered in the item-view pane.

3. Enter the text for the attachment.

4. Repeat steps 1 and 3 for each attachment.

5. Send or save the draft of the message as usual.

While working in an attachment, you may return to the original message or another attachment. Just select the icon for the original message or other attachment. When selected, an arrow appears before the icon, and the content of the attachment appears in the item-view pane.

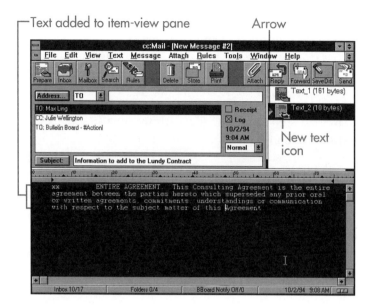

Figure 10.1   Creating text to attach to a message.

Attaching an Existing File

You can attach any existing file to a message. The file may
have been created by virtually any program that can run on a
personal computer. An attached file does not have to be a
file created with a Windows program.

To attach a file, follow these steps:

1. From the Message Window for a new message,
    open the Attach menu and choose Files. The dialog
    box shown in Figure 10.2 appears.

2. Use the pull-down lists to select the drive and directory of the file, and then select the file by name. Once the file name is displayed in the Files text box, select Add or double-click on the file. The file appears in the Attachments area.

3. Repeat step 2 until all files you want to attach are identified in the Attachments area.

4. Select OK.

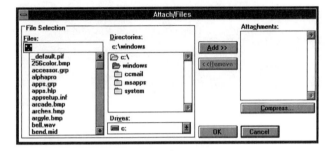

Figure 10.2 The Attach/Files dialog box.

Deleting Attachments If you inadvertently select a file in the Attach/Files dialog box that you don't want, you aren't stuck with it. In the Attachments list, highlight the file you want to remove and select Remove. Or if you have returned to the Message Window, highlight the attachment you don't want and press Del.

Attaching a Clipboard Item

You can also attach information from the Windows Clipboard to a cc:Mail for Windows message.

The Windows Clipboard   The Clipboard is a temporary storage location where information is stored when it is cut or copied. When you cut or copy new information, the contents of the Clipboard are replaced with the information most recently cut or copied. When you turn off your computer, the contents of the Clipboard are lost.

To attach an item with information from the Clipboard, you have to create your message and then switch to the application that contains the information you want to attach. After you copy the information to the Clipboard, you return to your message and complete the attachment. These are the steps in greater detail:

1.   Prepare your message using the cc:Mail Message Window.

2.   Click on the Control-menu box or press Alt+Spacebar. Select Switch To. From the Task List, select the application if it is open. If not, select the Windows Program Manager and then launch the application from which you want to copy or cut the data into the Clipboard.

3.   From inside the application, open the application file and copy the contents you want into the Clipboard. In most applications, you do this by highlighting the text and then selecting the Edit Copy command.

4.   Return to cc:Mail by selecting Switch To from the Control menu and then choosing cc:Mail.

5.   Back in the cc:Mail Message Window, select Clipboard from the Attach menu. The Clipboard Item Types dialog box appears (see Figure 10.3).

6. Enter the name you want to give to the attachment in the File Attachment Name text box (or keep the name that has been assigned). If the Clipboard contents were made up of text only, select Text for the Clipboard Item Types. If text and graphics were included in the Clipboard's contents, select All Item Types.

7. Select OK.

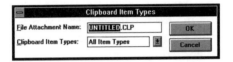

Figure 10.3   The Clipboard Item Types dialog box.

Avoid Confusion   When you create an attachment from Clipboard contents, you may want to use the .CLP file extension to distinguish the Clipboard attachment from the actual application files from which the attachment was taken.

Renaming an Attachment

To rename an attachment, select the attachment and then choose Rename Item(s) from the Message menu. Enter the new name in the Attachment Description dialog box. Select OK.

In this lesson, you learned how to create and rename attachments for your messages. In the next lesson, you will learn how to forward messages you receive to others.

Lesson

Forwarding Messages

In this lesson, you will learn how to forward messages to other parties.

Methods of Forwarding

The messages you receive may be useful for other people who were not on the TO or CC list. (Remember, blind carbon copies—BCCs—can be sent without your knowledge.)

You can forward a message from the Mailbox window or the Message Window. When forwarding a message from the Mailbox window, you can forward several messages at one time to the same recipient(s). When forwarding from the Message Window, however, you are restricted to forwarding only one message, but you have more control over changing information (such as content, subject, priority, return receipt, and attachments).

> **How to Address?** You will have to know how to enter addresses in order to forward messages. For a refresher, consult Lesson 3.

Forwarding from the Mailbox Window

Follow these steps to forward from the Mailbox window:

1. Select the message or messages to forward.

2. Press Ctrl+R or select Forward from the Message menu.

3. In the Address Message dialog box, enter the address information indicating the people or destinations for the forwarded message. Select Done.

4. In the Forward Information dialog box (see Figure 11.1), check the Retain Forwarding History check box to forward the message and include the original sender, subject, and send time. Deselect the check box to omit the header information.

5. Select Send to forward the message.

Figure 11.1   The Forward Information dialog box.

Forwarding from the Message Window

Although you can only forward a single message through the Message Window, the approach gives you more flexibility to control the message when it is forwarded. To forward, follow these steps:

1. Select the message to forward.

2. From the Message Window, press Ctrl+R or select Forward from the Message menu.

3. In the Forward Information dialog box, select Retain Forwarding History to forward the message and include the original sender, subject, and send time. Deselect it to omit the header information. Choose OK.

4. A message screen like that in Figure 11.2 appears. Enter the address, handling information, and subject. Type in any comments in the item-view pane. Change attachments and run the spell check, if desired.

5. Send the message by pressing Ctrl+S or selecting Send from the Message menu.

Header information

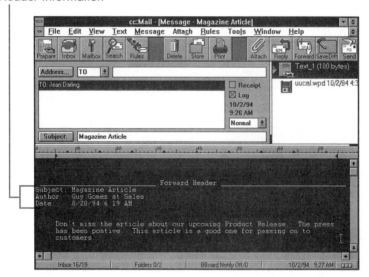

Figure 11.2 A message to forward complete with the header information in the item-view pane.

Ordering Comments Messages that have been forwarded one or more times can be confusing when it comes to separating original text from comments added later. A good approach is to add all comments at the top of the item-view pane area. This way, the most recent comments are immediately available, and the comments appear in order.

Reading a Message Forwarded to You

A message that has been forwarded looks a little different than a typical message. Figure 11.3 shows a forwarded message. The name of the person who forwarded the message appears after the **Fwd by...** button. You can select the button to see the Forwarding Information history.

Comments added   Forwarded by

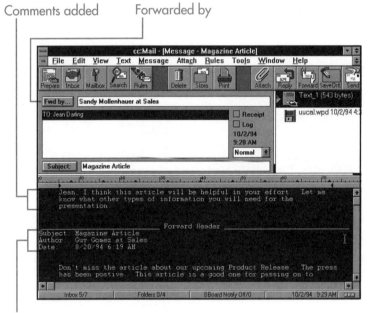

Header from original message

Figure 11.3 A forwarded message.

In this lesson, you learned two ways to forward a message. In the next lesson, you will learn how to reply to a message.

Lesson

Replying to a Message

In this lesson, you will learn how to save time in replying to messages.

Why Reply?

Using the reply features of cc:Mail for Windows saves you time addressing and composing messages. You can automatically address either the person who sent the message or all recipients, including the sender. Want to widen the scope of recipients? No problem. You can add recipients of your own. In addition, when you use the reply feature, you can add comments to the message that was sent to you or route a new message.

Replying to a Message

Follow these steps to reply to a message:

1. With the message to which you want to reply in the Message Window, open the Message menu and select Reply (or press Ctrl+Y).

2. The Reply dialog box shown in Figure 12.1 appears. Identify who you want to reply to (the Sender or All Addressees if there were multiple recipients). To keep the original message and attachments, check Retain the Original Items and then select Text Item or All.

3. The Reply Separator appears (see Figure 12.2). Add a reply or make any changes to this message.

4. Send the message by selecting Send from the Message menu.

Figure 12.1 The Reply dialog box.

Subject   Reply Separator

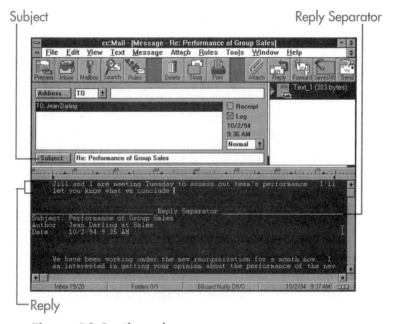

Reply

Figure 12.2 The reply message.

You may have noticed that the subject in Figure 12.2 was:

```
Re: Performance of Group Sales
```

The *Re:* was added by cc:Mail for Windows to indicate that this is a reply. If you send the reply, and your recipient replies back, a number is added in the subject area to indicate the second reply. For example,

```
Re[2]:
```

stands for the second reply to a message (in essence, a reply to your reply).

Adding and Editing Comments

When you enter a comment in the item-view pane, it's helpful for you to add it at the top. This way, the comment is readily available to the reader. Using different margins or a different color can also be helpful. Figure 12.3 illustrates the use of color. Here, a different color clearly identifies the comment and the edits that were made to the existing text.

Color Me Fuchsia   To use color to highlight text, select the text. Press the right mouse button (or press Ctrl+H). Apply the Pen Color. To change margins or tabs, select Margins/Tabs from the Text menu, and complete the Margins/Tabs dialog box. Lesson 4 covers adding color and changing margins in more detail.

Using color to add emphasis

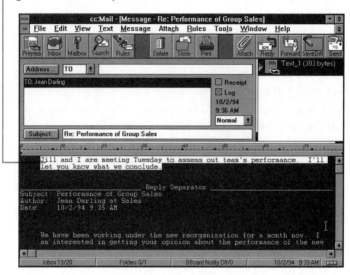

Figure 12.3 A reply with comments and edits in color.

In this lesson, you learned how to send replies to messages. In the next lesson, you will learn all about public and private mailing lists.

Public and Private Mailing Lists

In this lesson, you will learn how to create public and private mailing lists to make addressing messages easier.

Public Mailing Lists

When you address messages, you can use the cc:Mail for Windows Directory, public mailing lists, or private mailing lists. The Directory lists all individuals and destinations available to receive mail. Public and private mailing lists group people (possibly by department or work group) so that you don't have to address each person individually.

The cc:Mail Administrator creates public mailing lists. Figure 13.1 shows the expanded Mail List container with two public mailing lists.

Private Mailing List   A private mailing list is a list of up to 200 names created, maintained, and used by individual cc:Mail users. Public mailing lists are used to send mail to groups of people, thus streamlining the addressing of mail. The pound symbol (#) appears before the title of public mailing lists. Public mailing lists are available to multiple cc:Mail users. Only the cc:Mail Administrator can set up and change public mailing lists.

Expanding and Collapsing   Expand a Public or Private Mailing List container to see the available lists. Collapse a container to hide the lists. To expand or collapse, double-click on the container. Or select the container and then choose Expand or Collapse from the View menu.

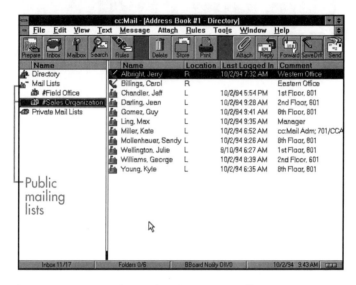

Figure 13.1   Public mailing lists: Field Office and Sales Organization.

Creating a Private Mailing List

Look at your private mailing lists as your own address books. You are responsible for the contents and organization. To create a private mailing list, follow these steps:

1.   Choose New Address Book from the Window menu.

2.   Expand and select the Private Mailing List container.

3.   Select New from the File menu.

4. In the Add New dialog box (shown in Figure 13.2), select Private Mailing List and then OK.

5. In the container pane, replace Untitled with the name for the new mailing list and press Enter.

Figure 13.2   The Add New dialog box for creating the Private Mailing List.

Adding Names to a Private Mailing List

To add addresses to the private mailing list at any time, follow these steps:

1. Select the list.

2. Choose File New.

3. In the Add New dialog box, select Mailing List Participants and choose OK.

4. The Participants List dialog box appears. Select the addresses as you did when you addressed messages. Then select Done.

> **Drag and Drop**   You can drag and drop names to a private mailing list. Select the Directory (or list you want to drag from). Make sure the Private Mailing List container appears in the container area. Drag the name to the container and release the mouse button.

Controlling a Private Mailing List

You can delete names in a private mailing list. Select the
name or names to delete and press Del (or select Delete from
the Edit menu). To delete the whole mailing list, select the
list and perform the same steps. A message appears asking
you to confirm deletion of the list.

To rename a private mailing list, select the private
mailing list. Open the File menu and choose Rename, or
press Ins. Type in the name you want to use and press Enter.

In this lesson, you learned how to create and control
private mailing lists. In the next lesson, you will learn how to
use folders and archives to help you manage all the mail you
receive.

Using Folders and Archives for Storage

In this lesson, you will learn how to use folders and archives to store your work and messages.

How Folders and Archives Differ

Folders and archives are places to store your messages. You can create up to 200 folders for exact indexing. Folders can be deleted and renamed, and messages in folders can be moved, copied, and deleted. You can have any number of archives. However, you don't want to store anything in an archive unless you know you won't need it again. You cannot access or manipulate anything stored in an archive.

> **Archive Cautions** Once you put a message in an archive, it cannot be moved or deleted from the archive. The archive itself can't be deleted or renamed; however, it can be removed from the contents pane. Archives are for permanent records.

Creating a Folder

To create a folder, follow these steps:

1. From the Mailbox window, select New from the File menu (or press Ctrl+N).

2. In the Add New dialog box (see Figure 14.1), select Folder and then select OK.

3. A new folder appears among existing folders (see Figure 14.2). At the cursor location, type in the title for the folder and press Enter.

Figure 14.1   The Add New dialog box.

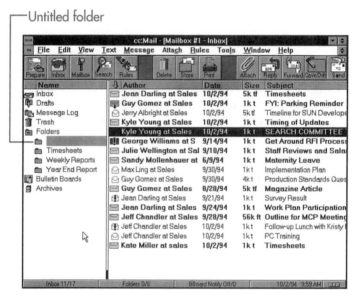

Figure 14.2   The Untitled new folder.

Creating an Archive

To create an archive, follow these steps:

1. From the Mailbox window, select File New (or press Ctrl+N).

2. In the Add New dialog box, select Archive (refer to Figure 14.1) and then choose OK.

3. The Create Archive dialog box appears (see Figure 14.3). Enter the drive and directory and an 8-character or less name for the new archive. Select OK.

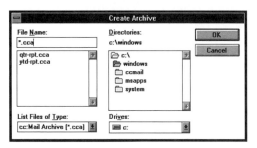

Figure 14.3   The Create Archive dialog box.

The Case of Archives   When you create an archive, you are creating a file. Archives cannot be distinguished by case. YTD-Rpt is the same as ytd-rpt. Archive names are displayed in lowercase regardless of what you enter.

Storing Messages

Messages can be copied or moved between containers with the Store command. The one exception is that messages cannot be moved out of an archive; cut and move options are simply not available.

Follow these steps to move or copy:

1. Select one or more messages.

2. Select Store from the File menu (or press Ctrl+T).

3. In the Store dialog box (shown in Figure 14.4), enter the name of the container or click on the container to highlight it. Identify the Action as Copy or Move.

4. Select OK. If a confirmation message appears, select OK.

Figure 14.4 The Store dialog box.

Fast Methods to Move or Copy Messages To move or copy a message from a list to a container, you can use the drag-and-drop method. You can also use cut-and-copy techniques. Both are described in Lesson 2.

Controlling Folders and Archives

To delete a folder (including all the messages), select it and press Del or choose Edit Delete. A confirmation message appears. Select OK. Remember, to delete an individual message from a folder, select the message and press Delete.

You cannot delete an archive or an individual archive message, but you can remove the name from the contents pane. Do this if you want to stop using the archive for future storage. Select the archive and press Del or select Edit Delete. A message asks you to confirm the deletion. The archive disappears, but the file remains on disk.

To rename a folder, select the folder and then choose Rename from the File menu, or press Ins. Type in the new name and press Enter. (Remember, you cannot rename archives.)

In this lesson, you learned how to use folders and archives to store your messages. In the next lesson, you'll learn how to find your messages among all the containers.

Lesson 15

Searching for What You Need

In this lesson, you will learn how to search out what you need using two different methods—quick search and the Search command.

Using Quick Search

When many messages are spread between a number of containers, you may need some help to find a specific item. The same is true as the address list grows and grows. Use quick search to find a single item in a sorted list. These include items in a container pane, a particular mailing list, or an address within the Directory or mailing list.

To use quick search, follow these steps:

1. Place your cursor in the list. (To search for an item in a container, you must expand the container by double-clicking on it or selecting View Expand.)

2. Type in a character. The Quick Search dialog box appears (see Figure 15.1), and the first occurrence of the character is highlighted.

3. Continue to type the word to refine the selection, or select Find Next to go to the next occurrence of the character(s) already entered.

4. Select Done when the search is complete.

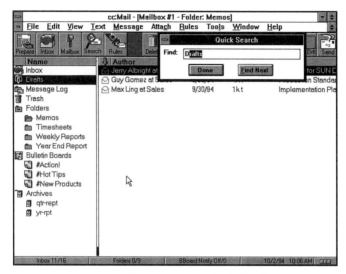

Figure 15.1   The Quick Search dialog box.

More Specific Searches

Quick search is limited to finding a single occurrence in a specific list. cc:Mail's more powerful Search command allows you to pinpoint exact messages or addresses. For example, you can find mail that has not been read, find messages according to the sender, date, or other header information, or even find an attachment.

When you perform a search, you'll use the Search dialog box shown in Figure 15.2.

Use the *search conditions pane* to identify what you want to find. You will use drop-down lists to make selections. The Find drop-down list allows you to choose whether you want to find a message or an address. The In drop-down list identifies the container to search. The If line allows you to set up logic to limit the search. For example, you might identify this information in the If line: If subject contains timesheets. cc:Mail will then search for messages with the subject timesheets. Or you might enter If unread is true to search for all unread messages.

Search conditions pane   Item pane

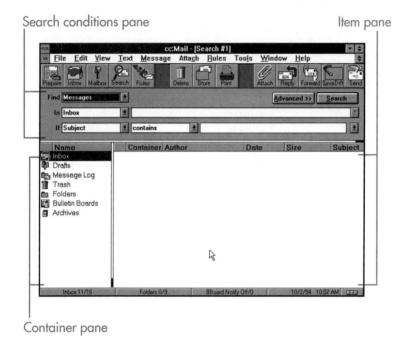

Container pane

Figure 15.2 The Search dialog box.

In the If line, when you change the selection in the first pull-down list, the remaining options change to match the first selection. Table 15.1 shows the If line options for both messages and addresses.

Table 15.1 Message and Address If line options.

If Selection	Comparison Selection	Setting Entry or Selection
For Messages:		
Subject	contains/does not contain/is/is not	Text you've entered
Text	contains/ does not contain	Text you've entered
Author (Sender)	contains/ does not contain/ is/is not	Name you've entered
Recipient (TO, CC, BCC)	contains/ does not contain/ is/is not	Name you've entered
TO	contains/ does not contain/ is/is not	Name you've entered
CC	contains/ does not contain/ is/is not	Name you've entered
BCC	contains/ does not contain/ is/is not	Name you've entered
Send date	is before/is after/ is/is not	Date you've entered
Send time	is before/is after/ is/is not	Date you've entered

continues

Table 15.1 Continued

If Selection	Comparison Selection	Setting Entry or Selection
For Messages:		
Age	is less than/ is more than/ is/is not	Number of days entered
Size (of file)	is less than/ is more than/ is/is not	Number of Kbytes entered
Priority	is/is not	Low/Normal/ Urgent
Item type (attachment)	includes/ does not include	Text/File/ Graphic/Fax
Item title (attachment)	contains/ does not contain/ is/is not	Text you've entered
Unread	is	True/False
Receipt Returned	is	True/False
For Addresses:		
Name	contains/ does not contain/ is/is not	Name you've entered
Location	is/is not	Local/Alias/ Remote user at post office/ Remote user/ Remote post office/Post office
Comment	contains/ does not contain/ is/is not	Text you've entered

If Selection	Comparison Selection	Setting Entry or Selection
For Addresses:		
Last logged-in date	is before/is after /is/is not /is empty/is not empty	Date you've entered
Last logged-in time	is before/is after /is/is not	Time you've entered

Performing the Search

To perform a search with the Search command, follow these steps:

1. Select Search from the Tools menu.

2. Complete each drop-down list in the Search dialog box conditions pane.

3. Click on the Search button or press Alt+S to find the message. The Search Status dialog box appears.

Once you find a message or other item, it appears in the *item pane* of the Search dialog box. The *container pane* appears to allow you to copy or move the item found to a container if you would like.

> **Forget How to Copy and Move?**   Use the drop-and-drag technique to copy or move a message or address. (Remember to press Ctrl when you drag to copy.) The **Copy**, **Cut**, and **Paste** commands in the **Edit** menu can also be used. Use the **Store** command from the **File** menu to move a message.

If the Search Is Wrong or Taking Too Long   Once you have started a search, you can stop it at any time by selecting Cancel.

In this lesson, you learned how to find a message or address using cc:Mail's two search methods. In the next lesson, you'll learn how to search more than one container using multiple conditions.

Lesson 16

Advanced Searches

In this lesson, you will learn how to perform advanced searches using the Search dialog box.

Advanced Search Steps

In the last lesson, you learned how to search one container with one line of conditions with cc:Mail's Search command. The same command can be used to search multiple containers and combine conditions. To perform such a search, follow these steps:

1. Open the Tools menu and select Search.

2. The Search dialog box appears. Instead of completing the search conditions, click on the Advanced button, or press Alt+A. The advanced conditions shown in Figure 16.1 appear.

3. Complete the search conditions.

4. Click on the Search button, or press Alt+S.

> **Return to Basic?** If you begin using the advanced search conditions and decide that the basic ones are for you, you don't have to start over. Click on the Basic button, or press Alt+B.

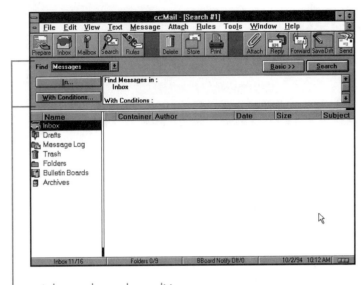

Advanced search conditions

Figure 16.1   Advanced search conditions window.

Using the Find Drop-Down List

The first advanced search condition is familiar. In the Find
drop-down list, you can select either Messages or Addresses.

Using the In Button

The In button is used to define the containers to search. For
maximum selection capability, expand all the containers by
selecting Expand All from the View menu. Then select the In
button. The Find Messages dialog box appears (see Figure 16.2).

In the Find Messages dialog box, use the Find Messages
in drop-down box to identify a container to search. When
you select certain containers, you can refine the search
further. For example, Figure 16.3 shows that you can select
all bulletin boards or a specific one. When you have identified the container using the drop-down lists, select Add. The
container then appears in the view/edit box. Continue to add

containers you want to search. Once the dialog box is complete and all containers appear in the view/edit box, select OK.

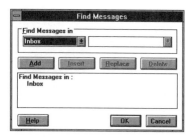

Figure 16.2   The Find Messages dialog box.

View/edit box —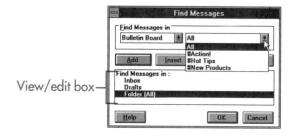

Figure 16.3   Refining folder selection.

Oops!   Even after you've added a container, you can change your mind. To remove the container, select it in the view/edit box of the Find Messages dialog box. Then choose the Delete button.

Using the With Conditions Button

Select the With Conditions button to specify the conditions of the search. When you select it, the Conditions dialog box appears. Figure 16.4 shows a completed Conditions dialog box with the conditions in the view/edit box. The search will select messages that meet all of these conditions:

- The send date is after 5/1/93

- AND Jeff Cochran is a TO recipient

- AND the priority is urgent

If OR were selected instead of AND, any messages meeting at least one of the above conditions would be selected.

View/edit box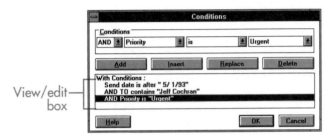

Figure 16.4 The completed Conditions dialog box.

Possible Conditions Refer to Table 15.1 in Lesson 15 to see the possible conditions that you can set.

To complete the Conditions dialog box, enter one line of conditions using the pull-down lists and text boxes. Then select Add. If desired, add another line of conditions. You will have to indicate whether the next line starts with AND (both conditions must be met) or OR (either condition can be met). Continue until all conditions are set. To delete a line of conditions, select the line and choose Delete. Choose OK when the Conditions dialog box is complete.

In this lesson, you learned how to extend your search to multiple containers and conditions. In the next lesson, you will learn how to change window settings.

Lesson

Changing Window Settings

In this lesson, you will learn how to permanently change the size, position, and look of cc:Mail SmartWindows.

Controlling Size and Position

You can control a window's size and location using the typical Microsoft Windows approaches. To size a window, select the Control-menu box and choose Size. Your cursor turns into a four-headed arrow. Resize the window as desired. Or you can use the mouse to drag the window's border. To move the entire window, select the window's Control-menu box and choose Move. Then place the cursor in the title bar and move the window. (Or you can drag the window's title bar with the mouse without using the Control-menu box.)

> **Selecting the Control-Menu Box** To open the Control-menu box for any window, you can press Alt and then the key shown in the box (in this example, the key is a hyphen). A faster way is to double-click on the box with the mouse.

Changing Pane Size and Column Widths

If you have a mouse, you can also change a window's pane size. Drag the pane-separator line (the line between panes) to the new location.

Many panes contain several columns. For example, Figure 17.1 shows the columns in the contents pane of the Mailbox window. The column headings are Author, Date, Size, and Subject.

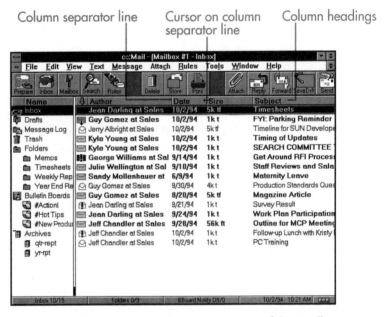

Figure 17.1 Columns in the contents pane of the Mailbox window.

You must have a mouse to control the width of columns in a pane. To change the width of a column, follow these steps:

1. Place the cursor on a column separator line. (The cursor appears as a two-headed arrow.)

2. Drag the column separator line to the new location.

Figure 17.2 shows the Mailbox window after some work. Here, the pane-separator line and the columns have been repositioned to reveal as much of the Subject column as possible. As you can see, this is a much better use of space than was the Mailbox window layout shown in Figure 17.1.

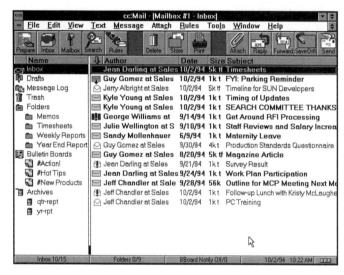

Figure 17.2   The Mailbox window after repositioning.

Changing Windows Defaults

When you move or size a window, change a window's pane size, or adjust pane columns, the changes you make are lost when you leave cc:Mail. You can permanently customize the following cc:Mail windows:

- Mailbox window
- Message window
- Address Book window
- Rules List window

You can also customize the Search dialog box and the Rule Editor dialog box. (Rules are covered in Lessons 19 and 20.)

If you want the changes to remain in place when you leave cc:Mail, follow these steps:

1. Double-click on the Control-menu box or press Alt+-.

2. Select Save Window Defaults Now to save the current settings for the window as the new default (even if you make other settings later). Or select Save Window Defaults on Exit to save the settings in place when you leave cc:Mail for Windows.

In this lesson, you learned how to change the size, position, and appearance of the windows. In the next lesson, you'll learn how to further customize cc:Mail for Windows.

Lesson

Customizing cc:Mail for You

In this lesson, you will learn how to customize cc:Mail for Windows to meet your needs.

Selecting User Setup Options

A variety of customizations can be performed from the User Setup dialog box. We won't cover them all, but we will cover those of importance to most users. For example, you may control the appearance of the desktop, change your password, control the notifications you are sent, set defaults for message handling, and control the Message Log, Trash, and Drafts containers.

Follow these steps to enter customizations:

1. Open the Tools menu and select User Setup.

2. The User Setup dialog box appears, as shown in Figure 18.1.

3. The Desktop icon is initially selected in the Preference list box. Make changes that affect the desktop or select another icon from the Preference list box to make changes.

4. The following sections describe the most common changes made in the User Setup dialog box. Make any of these changes you want. When you have entered all changes, select OK.

Preference list box

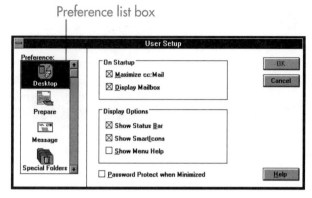

Figure 18.1 The User Setup dialog box.

The Desktop: cc:Mail's "Look"

You can enter settings to control the appearance of cc:Mail when you enter the program. Make sure the Desktop icon is selected in the Preference list box of the User Setup dialog box. You can customize the desktop by clicking on any of the check boxes described below.

- **Maximize cc:Mail:** Select for a full-size display. Deselect to save the size and position settings when you quit cc:Mail.

- **Display Mailbox:** Select to display the Mailbox window at startup.

- **Show Status Bar:** Select to display the status bar.

- **Show SmartIcons:** Select to display the SmartIcon palette.

- **Show Menu Help:** Select to have cc:Mail present information about menus and SmartIcons in the title bar.

- **Password Protect when Minimized:** cc:Mail can be minimized to an icon (consult Appendix A). When it is, select this check box and your password will be required to return to window size.

Changing Your Password

Speaking of passwords, it is a good idea to change your password regularly to ensure that only you have access to your mail. From the User Setup dialog box, select the Password icon from the Preference list box. Type in your Old Password and press Tab. Type in your New Password, press Tab, and then enter the New Password Again. Select OK.

Mail and Other Notifications

You may receive an unread mail notification when you start cc:Mail for Windows. The notification (covered in Lesson 7) tells you how many messages are unread. This and other notifications can be controlled. From the User Setup dialog box, select the Notify icon in the Preference list box. The options shown in Figure 18.2 appear.

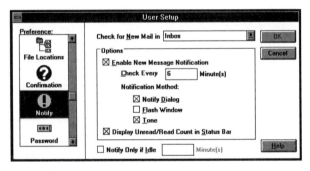

Figure 18.2 Notify options.

Set the notification for the inbox mail first. At Check for New Mail in, select Inbox. Then choose from these options:

- **Enable New Message Notification:** When you select this option, the messages in the container will be included in the new message notification. This option also allows you to specify how often cc:Mail for Windows checks for new mail. (Enter five minutes or more to keep network action down.)

You can also specify how you want to receive notification.

• Display Unread/Read Count in Status Bar: Select this check box to display on the status bar the number of read and unread messages.

Once you have entered the settings for the inbox, select Folders in the Check for New Mail in drop-down list. Enter those selections. Finally, select Bulletin Boards in the Check for New Mail in drop-down list and enter those settings. Choose OK when you are done.

Improving Message Handling

Message handling can be customized to your needs. Choose the Message icon in the Preference list box of the User Setup dialog box. The options shown in Figure 18.3 appear.

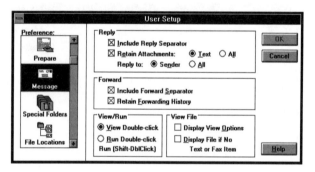

Figure 18.3   Message options.

There are four major message handling settings that you can control. A description of each follows.

• Reply: Identify the reply defaults, including whether to include a reply separator, whether to retain only text attachments or all attachments, and who to reply to.

- Forward: Specify whether to include a separator and whether to retain history on messages you forward.

- View/Run: Indicate what happens when you double-click an attachment.

- View File: Tell cc:Mail how to handle files that are attached to a message.

Settings for the Message Log, Trash, and Drafts

Select the Special Folders icon in the Preference list box to control the Message Log, Trash, and Drafts. You can indicate whether you want cc:Mail to automatically delete messages from your Message Log. If you do, specify how long to keep messages before they are deleted. For Trash, you can tell cc:Mail when to empty the Trash container. Finally, you can specify whether to allow the saving of draft messages.

Controlling the New Message Window

You can select the Prepare icon in the User Setup dialog box to control how the New Message window works for you. The Start Prepare in selections allow you to identify the cursor's starting location. You can choose Subject area, Text Editor, Addressing (to access the Address text box), Addressing Dialog (to access the Address Message dialog box), or Attach Dialog (to access the Attach/Files dialog box).

Among the Defaults check boxes, check Enable Message Log to send a copy of your messages to the Message Log. Check Request Receipt if you want a receipt. Check Automatic Spell Check if want to have cc:Mail automatically run the spell checker every time you send a new, forwarded, or reply message.

For the Address options, you can indicate whether you want the default to be TO, CC, or BCC. Finally, you can set the default priority as Urgent, Normal, or Low. Remember, these are just defaults. You can change the settings in individual messages for that message only.

Once all changes are entered, select OK.

Setting File Locations

In the User Setup dialog box, you can select the File Locations icon in Preferences to specify default directories. What directories? Those used for files that are attached, saved, archived, or imported/exported. Once you have selected the File Locations icon, select the Paths for drop-down list. Identify the files for which you will enter information (such as Attach Files, Save Files, and so on). Next, enter the path itself. You can type the path in the text box at the top of the Options area, or select the Browse button and then choose the path. Finally, choose from these option buttons:

- Use this Directory as Default (to always use the directory as the default).

- Remember Last Working Directory (to change the path default information to the path entered when you last performed the activity).

Continue to enter paths for all the types of files you'll handle. When you change the Paths for display, a confirmation appears showing changes made to the last chosen Paths for. Once you have entered all the paths you want, select OK.

Confirm?

cc:Mail for Windows has certain confirmations built in.

Confirmations   A *confirmation* is a message
that appears automatically asking you to confirm
that you want to complete the action you've
initiated. For example, when you delete a message, a confirmation window appears. It indicates
the deletion is about to take place and asks you to verify
the action.

You may want to add confirmations (to slow yourself
down before completing an action) or remove confirmations
(to speed your work when you aren't concerned about
making a mistake). To control whether you see a confirmation, from the User Setup dialog box, select the Confirmation
icon in Preferences. A series of check boxes appears. Place a
check in each check box to enable the confirmation (have it
appear). Leave the check box unchecked to disable the
confirmation (cause it not to appear).

Controlling Fonts

You can set new default fonts for text that appears in messages on your screen, printed messages, container lists,
address/message lists, and attachment lists. To affect the
fonts, select the Fonts icon in Preferences on the User Setup
dialog box. In Select Font, identify the text to affect. Then
select the Change Font button. In the Font dialog box, select
the Font, Font Style, and Size. Select OK when the Sample
appears. In the User Setup dialog box, select the Apply
button. Then continue to enter font changes to other Select
Font alternatives. Select OK in the User Setup dialog box
when you are completely finished.

A Font Limitation   As discussed in Lesson 4,
only monospaced fonts can be used. *Monospaced
fonts* are those fonts where each letter, number,
and symbol takes up the same amount of space.

Spell Check

Lesson 6 described how to spell check a document, including the use of two dictionaries. You can use the cc:Mail dictionary to check your spelling, or you can create and add words to your own personal dictionary. Through the User Setup dialog box, you can control the location of these dictionaries and the languages used. Select the Spell Check icon in Preferences.

In the Main Dictionary Directory text box, enter the location of the dictionary you want to use to perform spell check. After Language, select one of the languages in the list. Finally, enter the path and name for your personal dictionary in the User Dictionary text box. Select OK when you have completed all options.

Rules

Lessons 19 and 20 describe how to use cc:Mail rules to set up activities to automatically reoccur or be manually run. Those lessons cover how to create and use rules in detail. For now, just be aware that certain rule defaults can be changed through the User Setup dialog box. When you select the Rules icon in Preferences, you can check several check boxes to control the following rule options:

- Confirm to Execute a Rule: Requires a confirmation from you before a rule is run.

- Confirm to Delete a Rule: Requires a confirmation from you before a rule is deleted.

- Notify after Execution: Notifies you when a rule is run.

- Prefix Subject with "Rule:" when Rule Sends Message: Automatically adds the prefix "Rule:" to the subject of any message generated by a rule.

- Update Event Log
  c:\windows\ccmail\cc1dir\ccrule.log: Keeps a log of
  rules that are run; the log is saved as the ASCII file
  indicated (such as ccrule.log).

- Delete if File Size is Greater than *n* Kbytes: Identifies
  how large the file can grow before it is automatically
  deleted. To keep the file indefinitely, enter zero.
  Otherwise, enter the size in Kbytes (a Kbyte equals
  about 1000 characters). Type in the number of
  Kbytes in the Delete if File Size is Greater than in
  Kbytes text box.

In this lesson, you learned how to customize many of
cc:Mail for Windows' settings. In the next lesson, we'll turn
to a new subject—rules.

Making It Happen with Rules

In this lesson, you will learn how to get actions started using rules.

What Rules Can Do

You can set up cc:Mail for Windows rules to automate activities that you would otherwise perform manually.When you think about how you want to use rules, consider those activities you perform often and would like to automate. Here are some examples. You might want to copy specific messages from a Bulletin Board to your inbox automatically on startup. You might want to forward messages from one person to another automatically. You might want to develop a rule to empty your Trash folder when you leave cc:Mail for Windows. Or before leaving for an extended personal leave, you might want to draft a message to be sent to everyone who sends you mail during your absence. These activities and many more can be set up by using rules.

Elements of a Rule

A rule is made up of:

- A name or description which identifies the rule.

- A scheduled run time that identifies whether the rule will be activated manually or automatically (and, if automatically, when it is activated).

- A list of the containers to search to find messages.

- The set of search conditions to perform on the container in order to find the desired messages.

- The action to perform that identifies what to do with the messages found.

Creating a Rule

To create a rule, follow these steps:

1. Select Rules List from the Rules menu. The Rules List window appears (see Figure 19.1).

2. Select Create New Rule from the Rules menu. The Rule Editor dialog box appears (see Figure 19.2).

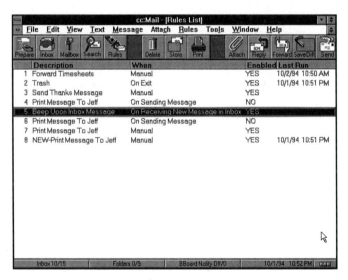

Figure 19.1 The Rules List window.

3. Enter the Description.

4. Indicate When to Run by selecting from the drop-down list.

5. Define the rule conditions by choosing the Find
Messages in button. In the Find Messages dialog
box, Add the containers to search and select OK.
Then select the With Conditions button and enter
the conditions. Finally, select the Action button and
complete the actions required for the specific rule.

6. When all information is complete in the Ruler Editor
dialog box, select Save. The rule appears in the
Rules List.

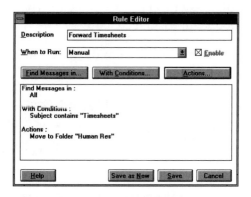

Figure 19.2 The Rule Editor dialog box.

For example, the rule defined in Figure 19.2 will be run
manually. All messages with the word Timesheets in the
subject will be moved to the folder named Human Res.

Need Help After Selecting a Button?
Using the dialog box after you select a button in
the Rule Editor dialog box involves the same steps
used to perform searches. You will select a container, condition, or action from the drop-down list and
then select the Add button. To delete a selection, choose
that selection and then choose the Delete button. For
more information, see Lessons 15 and 16.

Watch the Order   Always use the buttons in the Rule Editor dialog box from left to right when you create a rule. The **A**ctions are entered last and may vary depending on the earlier information you enter. Also, certain actions require more information to complete than others.

Once you've created a rule, you will want to test it to make sure it works as you anticipated. Otherwise, you may think a rule is in place, but it may not be functioning as expected.

Running Rules Manually

Some rules, like our example, are set up to run manually. You select the Manual setting in the **W**hen to run drop-down list in the Rule Editor dialog box when you create the rule. To run a rule manually, follow these steps:

1. Open the Rules menu and select Rules List.

2. From the Rules List window, select the Run Rule command in the Rules menu.

Running Rules Automatically

When a rule is created, you can run it automatically. Using the Ruler Editor dialog box, you can indicate that you want to run a rule when you send a message or upon cc:Mail startup by selecting one of these options in the **W**hen to Run drop-down list. For example, Figure 19.3 shows the setup that tells cc:Mail to delete the Trash container automatically upon exit from cc:Mail for Windows.

You can confirm that the rules identified to run automatically will run as scheduled. To do this, open the Rules menu and make sure Run Rules as Scheduled is checked. Deselect the command, and the rules set up to run automatically will not be run.

Figure 19.3   Trash deleted upon exit.

In this lesson, you learned how to create and run a rule. In the next lesson, you will learn how to change an existing rule.

Lesson

Controlling Rules

In this lesson, you will learn how to control existing rules.

Enabling and Disabling

You can enable or disable an existing rule.

Enable/Disable Enabling a rule means that you make the rule active, and it can be run manually or automatically according to the way the rule is set up. Disabling a rule means the rule is taken out of action. It cannot be run manually or automatically.

For example, let's say you have a rule that automatically moves messages with the subject AM Project from your inbox to the trash. But then you are asked to follow the project, so you want to temporarily stop the trashing of the messages. You could edit the rule to make it run manually, and then never run the rule. However, it is easier to stop a rule by disabling it. That way, if you want the rule to run again, you can just enable it rather than having to edit the rule.

To enable or disable a rule, follow these steps:

1. Select Rules List from the Rules menu.

2. Highlight the rule that you want to enable or disable.

3. From the Rules menu, choose Enable Rule or Disable Rule.

The status of the rule appears in the Rules List in the Enable column. Notice that in Figure 20.1, one rule is disabled: NO appears in the Enabled column. The other rules are enabled: YES appears in the Enabled column.

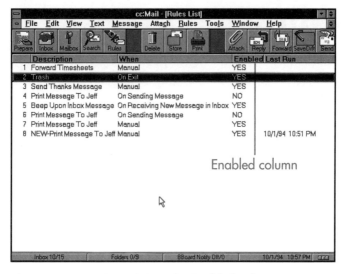

Figure 20.1   Yes or No in the Enabled column.

Editing or Copying a Rule

You can change an existing rule or make a copy of a rule. To do so, follow these steps:

1. Select Rules List from the Rules menu.

2. Double-click on the rule, or select it and press Enter. The Rule Edit dialog box appears.

3. Make any changes you would like.

4. Select Save to save the rule with the changes or select Save as New to make a new copy of the rule while maintaining the original rule.

Just A Copy Please   You can make a copy
of the rule without editing it by following the
previous steps without adding any edits.

Moving a Rule

You can move a rule from its position on the Rules List window. Moving a rule is useful to organize a long list of rules.
For example, you may want to put all manually run rules first
so they are easy to find. Automatically running rules could be
next and rules that are disabled last on the list.

In the Rules List window, highlight the rule to move.
Select Move Rule Position from the Rules menu. The Move
Rule dialog box appears (see Figure 20.2). Enter the new
position for the rule (numbered from the top of the list) and
select OK. The rule is immediately repositioned on the list.

Figure 20.2   The Move Rule dialog box.

Deleting a Rule

Deleting old rules prevents you from accidentally enabling
them and keeps your Rules List free from clutter. To delete a
rule, highlight the rule in the Rules List window. Choose the
Edit Delete command or press Del.

Before You Delete   Before you delete a rule,
be certain that you no longer need the rule. If you
are not certain, simply disable the rule and move
it to the bottom of the Rules List for possible future
use.

In this lesson, you learned how to control rules you've created. In the next lesson, you will learn how to customize SmartIcon sets.

Lesson

Customizing SmartIcon Sets

In this lesson, you will learn how to change the appearance of SmartIcons, display other SmartIcon sets, and create your own SmartIcon sets.

Changing the Size of SmartIcons

When you install cc:Mail, the default SmartIcon set appears. cc:Mail for Windows sets the size according to your monitor setup.

What Is a SmartIcon Set? We've learned that a SmartIcon is a button that you can click on to perform an operation. A *SmartIcon set* is simply the set of buttons that appear together on-screen.

You can change the display size of the SmartIcon set, making it appear small without text, large without text, or large with text. To change the size of SmartIcons, follow these steps:

1. Choose SmartIcons from the Tools menu.

2. In the SmartIcons dialog box (see Figure 21.1), select the Icon Size button.

3. Choose from Small, Large, or Large with Text.

4. Select OK.

Available icons   Current SmartIcon set

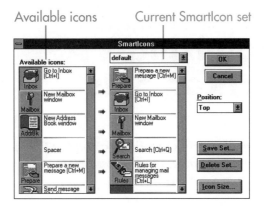

Figure 21.1 The SmartIcons dialog box.

Going for a Scroll? You can't scroll through
the SmartIcon buttons (except when you are viewing them in the SmartIcons dialog box). But you
can have more SmartIcons in a SmartIcon set than
appear on-screen. If there are too many SmartIcons to
see, scroll through the current SmartIcon set in the
SmartIcons dialog box to verify the contents. If some of
the SmartIcons don't appear and the set is displayed
as large, decrease the set to small. If all the SmartIcons
in the set still don't appear, you need to reduce the size
of the SmartIcon set or change the position to Floating
(see the next section).

Changing the Position of SmartIcons

The location in which SmartIcons are displayed can also be
changed. The default position is Top. (SmartIcons appear at
the top of the screen right under the menu bar.) However,

you can change the Position to Left, Right, Bottom (above the status bar), or Floating. If you select Floating, the SmartIcons appear in a movable, adjustable window.

The Floating position allows you to display more SmartIcons than does any other position. For example, the Top, Left, Right, and Bottom positions display only a single line of SmartIcons. The Floating position allows you to display more than one line. Also, by dragging, you can move a floating SmartIcon set almost all the way off the screen. This increases the display area for other uses.

To change the position of a SmartIcon set, follow these steps:

1. Select Tools SmartIcons.

2. In the SmartIcons dialog box, select a position from the Positions drop-down list.

3. Select OK.

Now You See It, Now You Don't!   When you choose to display SmartIcons in the Floating position, a close box appears in the upper left corner of the SmartIcons floating window. If you select the close box, the SmartIcon set disappears. To get them to reappear, select User Setup from the Tools menu. Select the Desktop Preference and check Show SmartIcons.

Displaying Other SmartIcon Sets

You might want to display a SmartIcon set other than the one currently displayed. Several SmartIcon sets come with cc:Mail, and (as discussed later) you can create SmartIcon sets of your own. Regardless of the number of SmartIcon sets you have, you can display only one at a time.

To display another SmartIcon set, click the Switch SmartIcon to display the next SmartIcon set. Or use these steps to display a different SmartIcon set:

1. From the Tools menu, select SmartIcons.

2. In the SmartIcons dialog box, select the drop-down list in the center of the dialog box (it holds the name of the currently displayed SmartIcon set).

3. Choose the name of the SmartIcon set you want to display.

4. Select OK.

Creating and Editing SmartIcon Sets

You can create a new SmartIcon set or edit an existing one. Follow these steps to do so:

1. Select SmartIcons from the Tools menu.

2. Display the set you want to edit or the set most like the one you want to create. To display a set, select it from the drop-down list in the center of the SmartIcons dialog box.

3. Change the selected SmartIcon set as desired.

    • Add a SmartIcon by dragging it from the Available icons shown on the left of the dialog box to the position desired in the SmartIcon set.

    • Delete a SmartIcon by dragging it off the SmartIcon set.

    • Move a SmartIcon from one position in the set to a new position by dragging the SmartIcon.

4. When you are finished editing, select the Save Set button. The Save Set dialog box appears.

5. In the Save Set dialog box (see Figure 21.2), you can replace the old SmartIcon set contents with the new by keeping the Name of set and File name as is. (A warning message appears before the new contents replace the old.) Or to create a new set and leave the old set alone, you can change the Name of set and the File name.

6. Select OK.

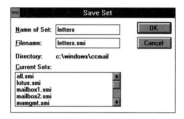

Figure 21.2   The Save Set dialog box.

Gimme Space!   You may notice the Spacer among the Available icons. Use it to create visual spaces between SmartIcons. You can add the Spacer to a SmartIcon set by dragging it to the desired position. Once it's in a set, you can move or delete a Spacer just like any SmartIcon. One Spacer takes up one half the space of a regular SmartIcon.

Delete a SmartIcon Set

Housekeeping is always important. Avoid confusion—don't clutter your SmartIcon sets with names of sets you no longer use.

To delete a SmartIcon set, select SmartIcons from the Tools menu. You will need to know the name of the SmartIcon set to delete. If you want to verify the name and contents of a SmartIcon set before you delete it, use the drop-down list in the center of the SmartIcons dialog box to display the SmartIcon set. Once you are sure of the name of the set to delete, select the Delete Set button. The Delete Sets dialog box appears with each set listed. Select the set to delete and choose OK.

In this lesson, you learned how to control and change SmartIcon sets. In the next lesson, you'll begin to learn how cc:Mail Mobile may be used to send and receive mail from remote locations.

Lesson

22

Mobile: Creating Messages

In this lesson, you will learn how to start cc:Mail Mobile and how to create and address messages.

With cc:Mail Mobile you can send and receive mail from remote locations (such as your home, another office, or a hotel room). Simply make a connection to the LAN before sending or receiving mail. You can also use cc:Mail Mobile in your office when the network is not operational, and then send and receive mail when the network becomes available again.

> **Be Sure to Share** Before installing cc:Mail Mobile, type **SHARE** at the DOS prompt. Or, better yet, add the line **SHARE.EXE** to your AUTOEXEC.BAT file so that SHARE loads automatically each time you start your computer.

Install cc:Mail Mobile following the same instructions you use for cc:Mail for Windows (see the inside front cover). Use the login name, password, post office name, post office phone number, and communication method supplied by your cc:Mail Administrator.

Once cc:Mail Mobile is installed, follow these steps to start it:

1. If you haven't loaded SHARE yet, type **SHARE** at the DOS prompt before starting Windows.

2. Start Windows by typing `win` at the DOS prompt.

3. From the Program Manager, select Lotus Applications and choose the cc:Mail Mobile icon (shown in Figure 22.1). The cc:Mail Login dialog box appears.

Figure 22.1 The cc:Mail Mobile icon.

4. In the cc:Mail Login dialog box (see Figure 22.2), always enter the correct Log-in Name, Password, and P.O. Path (post office), and select the Mode. (You can change the Location Name from within cc:Mail Mobile.)

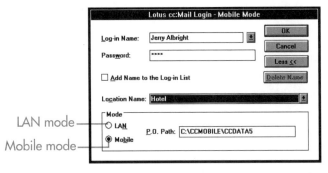

Figure 22.2 Choose between LAN mode and Mobile mode.

Each time you start up cc:Mail Mobile, you have the choice of working in LAN mode or Mobile mode (see Figure 22.2). LAN mode stands for Local Area Network mode; it is similar to regular cc:Mail for Windows and should be used when you are attached to the local network. Choose Mobile mode when you will occasionally communicate with the network to send or receive mail.

> **You Can Share** If you share your computer with another cc:Mail Mobile user, you can add that person when starting cc:Mail Mobile. In the Login dialog box, access the Log-in Name text box, enter the name, and choose the Add Name to the Log-in List check box. Complete the rest of the dialog box and choose OK. A message appears stating that no post office is found. Choose OK to create a new post office.

> **Limit Password Changes Between Sessions** To protect access to your mail, you can change your password following the steps covered in Lesson 18. However, don't change your password more than twice between communication sessions with your home post office. (The LAN uses your current and last two passwords for identification.)

Special Mobile Features

Most cc:Mail features are the same whether you're using Mobile or LAN mode. However, there are some special Mobile features to facilitate communication. Figure 22.3 highlights the additions to the cc:Mail Mobile screen.

The title bar reminds you whether you are working in Mobile or LAN mode. The Outbox in the container pane stores items you create in Mobile mode until they're sent. (In LAN mode, items are sent immediately.) The Session Log stores recorded communications and message information. The status bar tells you the location set up for transmission. Finally, the Mobile menu (which is new) provides a single point for sending and receiving remotely.

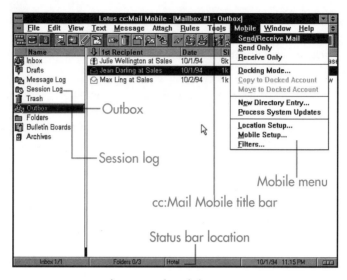

Figure 22.3   The cc:Mail Mobile screen.

Creating Messages

Whether you're working in Mobile mode or LAN mode, or using regular cc:Mail, create a message by opening the Message menu and selecting New Message. (See Lesson 3 to review creating a message.) When you select Send from the Message menu in Mobile mode, the message is placed in your Outbox for later communication.

Working with Your Address Book

With Mobile, you have a Directory for your Address Book. The cc:Mail Administrator might send the home Directory to your cc:Mail post office. (The Administrator can do this automatically with Automatic Directory Exchange. All you need to do is select Process System Updates from the Mobile menu to update your Directory.)

You can change or delete an Address Book entry by selecting the Window menu and choosing New Address Book Window. To delete an entry, highlight the entry, press

Delete, and follow the prompts. To change an entry, double-
click on the entry. Use the Directory Entry dialog box to
make changes, and then select OK.

Adding Directory Entries for Your Home Post Office

You can add directory entries for users at your home post
office by following these steps:

1. Select New Directory Entry from the Mobile menu.

2. Enter a name in the Name field and enter a Com-
    ment, if desired. (By default, the Directory Type is
    set to User, the Address Type is set to Directory
    Entry, and the Address is set to your home post
    office.)

3. Select OK. When you create a message and select
    Address, the entry appears in the Address Message
    window.

> **Drag and Drop**   You can quickly add an
> entry to your Mobile Directory by dragging a
> recipient's address from a message you've
> received to the Address Book window. To do this,
> open the message and choose New Address Book
> Window from the Window menu (reposition the windows
> if necessary for viewing). Then drag and drop.

Adding Directory Entries for Other Post Offices

You can add directory entries for users at post offices other
than your own home post office by following these steps:

1. Select New Directory Entry from the Mobile menu.

2. Complete the Directory Entry dialog box.

3. To enter a phone number, change the Address Type to Phone, and then enter the Country, Area/City, and Local Number. (See Figure 22.4.)

4. Finally, choose Add and click OK to complete the phone number operation.

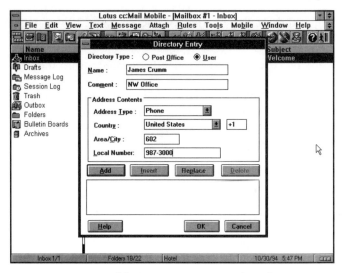

Figure 22.4 Adding Directory Entries for other Post Offices.

To deliver the message to your home post office so that it can be forwarded to another post office, select Directory Entry as the Address Type, use the default Address, and enter the name of the post office in the Address text box.

I Entered the Number! Simply entering a phone number in the Directory Entry dialog box might not give cc:Mail Mobile enough information to carry out the call. Any Address Type you enter must have communications set up through the Location Setup option on the Mobile menu (covered in more detail in the next lesson).

In this lesson, you learned how to start cc:Mail Mobile. You also learned how to create messages and address them to your post office or another post office. In the next lesson, you'll learn how to send and receive messages.

Lesson

23

Mobile: Sending and Receiving Mail

In this lesson, you will learn how to send and receive mail using cc:Mail Mobile.

Sending and Receiving Messages

When you choose Send from the Message menu while in Mobile mode, the message is stored in the Outbox until you connect to the post office. (In LAN mode, the message is immediately sent.) You can open your Outbox at any time to look at, copy, or delete messages.

Using the Mobile menu, you can send mail, receive mail, or send and receive mail in one operation. For example, you might want to receive your mail, review it, and update messages in your Outbox before sending them.

Follow these steps to send and/or receive messages:

1. Make sure the location from which you are transmitting appears in the status bar. If not, click on the location in the status bar and choose the appropriate location.

2. Open the Mobile menu and select Send/Receive Mail, Send Only, or Receive Only. The cc:Mail Background window appears to inform you of the progress of the communication.

cc:Mail Background   cc:Mail Background is your mail carrier. It transports your mail when communications are established.

Once you send the messages, they are deleted from the Outbox. Any message that couldn't be sent (for example, if the address was wrong), remains in the Outbox. A message appears to tell you that There are still messages in the Outbox to be sent.

No Go   If your mail is not sent, but all addresses and communications options are correct, try the communication again. Note any on-screen messages that might be important for troubleshooting, and contact your cc:Mail Administrator.

Viewing and Editing Location Profiles

Instructions on how to send the mail are attached to the location chosen in the status bar. For example, when you send mail from your home location, cc:Mail Mobile may dial only the number of your post office. If you send mail from an office location, cc:Mail Mobile might dial a 9 followed by the number. Each location has a location profile which describes all the associated settings.

To view the location profiles currently set up:

1.   Select Location Setup from the Mobile menu.

2.   If necessary, click on More>> to view the entire Location Setup dialog box shown in Figure 23.1.

Because Telephone is selected in Figure 23.1, the dialog box displays the rules for dialing from a hotel telephone. The rules include dialing 8, 1 for long distance, the area code, and the number. Select Communications to identify the type of communication method used (such as a modem and related settings). Choose Schedule to identify the time and frequency of automatic sending and receiving.

Telephone selection   New button   Hotel location

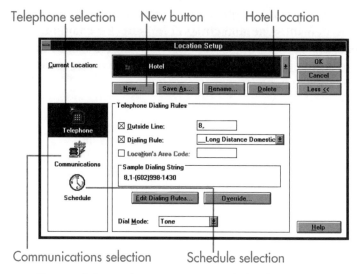

Communications selection   Schedule selection

Figure 23.1   The Location Setup dialog box.

　　To edit any settings for current locations, make your changes and select OK. Using the Save **As**, **R**ename, or Delete buttons, you can save a profile under a new name, rename an existing profile, or delete a profile. You can also create a new location profile by selecting the New button in the Location Setup dialog box and proceeding.

> **Don't Be Confused!**   Some location profile settings can be confusing. This is especially true if you are calling foreign countries, using a calling card, or using connections other than via a modem. Don't hesitate to enlist the help of your cc:Mail Administrator when changing or creating new location profiles.

Filtering Your Messages

You may want to filter your messages to select only the messages you specify. For example, you might have limited storage space and want to accept messages only up to a certain size. Or, you might want to receive and dispose of priority items first or items from certain senders. Filtering reduces the amount of storage space required and also lowers connection time (and possibly long distance costs).

The filters you set up are used for each incoming message until you change them. Follow these steps to add filters:

1. Select Filters from the Mobile menu. The Filters dialog box shown in Figure 23.2 appears.

2. Check the check box of each filter you want to apply (the filters are described in the next section), and enter the filter criteria in the text box.

3. When you have chosen all appropriate filters, choose OK.

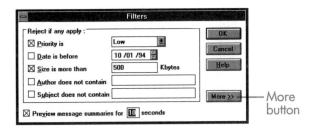

Figure 23.2   The Filters dialog box.

The following list describes each of the filter options available in the Filters dialog box:

- The **Priority is** filter rejects low priority items when Low is selected, and rejects both Low and Normal priority items when Normal is selected.

- The **Date is before** filter rejects items sent before the date you specify.

- The **Size is more than** filter rejects items greater than the size in kilobytes (Kbytes) that you specify in the text box.

- The **Author does not contain** filter rejects all messages except those from the author or post office you specify. For an author, you can enter the first and/or last name. Messages with names that match any part of your entry are not rejected.

- The **Subject does not contain** filter rejects all messages unless the specified word(s) are included in the subject. Messages that contain any sequence that matches your entry are not rejected.

- The **Preview message summaries for** *nn* **seconds** filter tells cc:Mail Mobile to display message summaries for the number of seconds you specify. You can choose to **Accept Message** or **Reject Message** based on the summary. You can also choose **Stop** to terminate the connection. If you don't accept or reject a message within the timeframe, the message is accepted automatically.

> **Filtered but Still Waiting** Messages that are filtered and rejected remain in your LAN Inbox. You can dispose of them later in either Mobile or LAN mode.

Select the More>> button in the Filters dialog box to display an area in which to set up filters using Rules (Figure 23.3 shows this option). Choose New to create a new rule, or choose Edit to edit an existing rule. The Rule Editor dialog box appears.

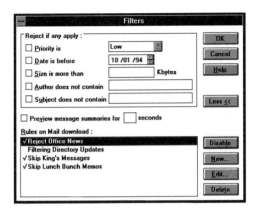

Figure 23.3   The Filters dialog box with the Rules area displayed.

Once a rule is in place, you can select the rule and choose Enable or Disable to activate or deactivate the rule. (A check mark appears before a rule that is enabled.) Choose Delete to remove a rule. Review Lessons 19 and 20 for more information on using rules.

Using Docking Mode

While physically connected to the LAN, you can copy or move messages between the LAN and your Mobile mailbox using docking mode. By doing so, you can manage message storage while in your local office.

> **Everything In Its Place**   To use docking mode, you must have login accounts for both LAN and Mobile modes on your portable computer, and the computer must be connected by cable to the LAN.

To use docking mode, follow these steps:

1. Start cc:Mail Mobile by logging in to the mode from which you want to transfer mail. Display the items to copy or move.

2. From the Mobile menu, select Docking Mode.

3. Enter the required information in the cc:Mail Docking dialog box. Select the Mode to which you want to transfer mail and choose OK.

4. A Docking dialog box appears. Highlight the items you want to copy or move.

5. From the Mobile menu, choose Copy to Docked Account or Move to Docked Account.

6. When you are done, choose Exit Docking Mode from the Docking dialog box. When you see the message Exit docking mode?, select Yes.

In this lesson, you learned how to send and receive mail using cc:Mail Mobile, how to filter the mail you receive, and how to use docking mode. In the next lesson, you'll learn how to customize cc:Mail Mobile to streamline your work.

Lesson

Mobile: Customizing

In this lesson, you will learn how to make cc:Mail Mobile match your own requirements.

Mobile Setup

You can customize cc:Mail Mobile to create an exact fit. You can change information related to your home post office, enter calling card numbers, set up communication features, and reclaim storage space. To effect changes, follow these steps:

1. Select Mobile Setup from the Mobile menu. The Mobile Setup dialog box (shown in Figure 24.1) appears.

2. Enter customizations to meet your needs.

3. Choose OK.

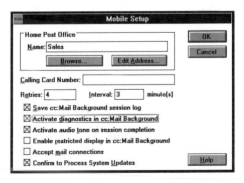

Figure 24.1 The Mobile Setup dialog box.

Your Home Post Office Settings

If your home post office changes, enter the new information in the Mobile Setup dialog box. You can enter a new Home Post Office **Name**. (If you select one using **B**rowse, the Location must be P for post office.) Or, select Edit Address to change the address of your home post office.

Entering a Calling Card Number

You can enter a calling card number in the Mobile Setup dialog box. Then, when you select a location with a Telephone Dialing Rule for **Calling Card Call**, the number you enter here is automatically used. (To review how to access the Telephone options when creating or editing locations, see Lesson 23.)

Retrying Your Connection

You can't always make a connection on the first try. For that reason, it is a good idea to set up cc:Mail Mobile to retry the communication. Simply enter the number of **R**etries and the **I**nterval (in minutes between retries) in the Mobile Setup dialog box.

Busy or Wrong?   If the phone number you're calling is busy, retrying will help ensure success. However, if the communications are set up wrong, no number of retries will establish a connection.

Getting Information About Your Sessions

Most of the check boxes in the Mobile Setup dialog box provide specific controls for communication sessions. You can check any of the following options:

- **S**ave cc:Mail Background session log: Saves information from each communications session to your Session Log.

- Activate diagnostics in cc:Mail Background: Saves additional technical information (such as modem strings and packet failures).

- Activate audio tone on session completion: Sounds a tone when the communication session is complete.

- Enable restricted display in cc:Mail Background: Stops cc:Mail Background from displaying potentially confidential information, such as post office names and addresses.

- Accept mail connections: Incoming mail communications are only accepted if cc:Mail Background is activated. (You don't have to be running cc:Mail Mobile.)

The final check box in the Mobile Setup dialog box is Confirm to Process System Updates. Check this option to have cc:Mail Mobile display a confirmation screen when system updates (such as a Directory update) are sent.

Running Only cc:Mail Background

You might want to run cc:Mail Background without cc:Mail Mobile to accept incoming mail (set up via the Mobile menu and then Mobile Setup) or to make scheduled calls (setup via the Mobile menu, Location Setup, and Schedule).

To run only cc:Mail Background, select Lotus Applications from the Windows Program Manager and choose the cc:Mail Background icon. Complete the usual information in the Login dialog box. The cc:Mail Background screen appears (see Figure 24.2). Select the Message Summary button (a check mark appears) to display the communication steps; check the Diagnostics button for technical information. Select Start to begin the communications session. Click on Stop at any time to halt the communication.

Xs indicates that Message
Summary and Diagnostics
are not selected.

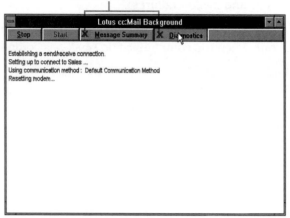

Figure 24.2 The cc:Mail Background screen.

WMREORG Utility

cc:Mail Mobile helps you recover empty and unused local
post office storage space automatically. When you can
recover storage space, cc:Mail Mobile displays a dialog box
notifying you to run the WMREORG utility. In response to
the dialog box, select OK. Several status windows appear,
followed by a dialog box indicating that WMREORG was
successful. Choose OK, and continue your work.

In this lesson, you learned how to customize cc:Mail
Mobile to meet your specific requirements. This lesson
concludes your guide. However, don't miss the inside back
cover, which provides a quick reference to the SmartIcons
for commonly used functions.

Appendix

Microsoft Windows Primer

Microsoft Windows is an interface program that makes your computer easier to use by enabling you to select menu items and pictures rather than type commands. Before you can take advantage of it, however, you must learn some Windows basics.

Starting Microsoft Windows

To start Windows, do the following:

1. At the DOS prompt, type `win`.

2. Press Enter.

The Windows title screen appears for a few moments, and then you see a screen like the one in Figure A.1.

> **What If It Didn't Work?** You may have to change to the windows directory before starting Windows; to do so, type `CD\WINDOWS` and press Enter.

Parts of a Windows Screen

As shown in Figure A.1, the Windows screen contains several unique elements that you won't see in DOS. Here's a brief summary.

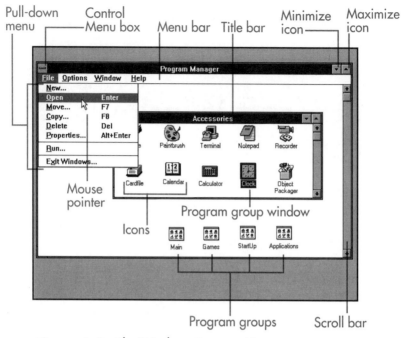

Pull-down menu | Control Menu box | Menu bar | Title bar | Minimize icon | Maximize icon

Mouse pointer

Icons   Program group window

Program groups   Scroll bar

Figure A.1 The Windows Program Manager.

- *Title bar* Shows the name of the window or program.

- *Program group windows* Contain program icons which allow you to run programs.

- *Icons* Graphic representations of programs. To run a program, you select its icon.

- *Minimize and Maximize buttons* Alter a window's size. The Minimize button shrinks the window to the size of an icon. The Maximize button expands the window to fill the screen. When maximized, a window contains a double-arrow *Restore* button, which returns the window to its original size.

- *Control-menu box* When selected, pulls down a menu that offers size and location controls for the window.

- *Pull-down menu bar*   Contains a list of the pull-down menus available in the program.

- *Mouse pointer*   If you are using a mouse, the mouse pointer (usually an arrow) appears on-screen. It can be controlled by moving the mouse (discussed later in this appendix).

- *Scroll bars*   If a window contains more information than it can display, you will see a scroll bar. *Scroll arrows* on each end of the scroll bar allow you to scroll slowly. The *scroll box* allows you to scroll more quickly.

Using a Mouse

To work most efficiently in Windows, you should use a mouse. You can press mouse buttons and move the mouse in various ways to change the way it acts:

Point means to move the mouse pointer onto the specified item by moving the mouse. The tip of the mouse pointer must be touching the item.

Click on an item means to move the pointer onto the specified item and press the mouse button once. Unless specified otherwise, use the left mouse button.

Double-click on an item means to move the pointer onto the specified item and press and release the left mouse button twice quickly.

Drag means to move the mouse pointer onto the specified item, hold down the mouse button, and move the mouse while holding down the button.

Figure A.2 shows how to use the mouse to perform common Windows activities, including running applications and moving and resizing windows.

Click to control
size and location.— Drag title bar to
move window.   Click to
shrink.—   Click to
expand.

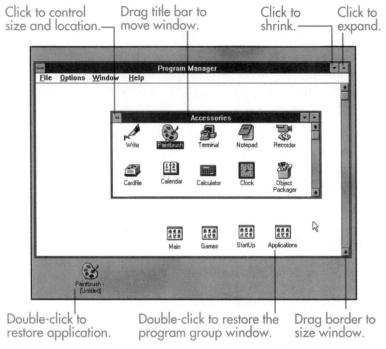

Double-click to
restore application.   Double-click to restore the
program group window.   Drag border to
size window.

Figure A.2 Use your mouse to control Windows.

Starting a Program

To start a program, simply select its icon. If its icon is contained in a program group window that's not open at the moment, open the window first. Follow these steps:

1. If necessary, open the program group window that contains the program you want to run. To open a program group window, double-click on its icon.

2. Double-click on the icon for the program you want to run.

Using Menus

The pull-down menu bar (see Figure A.3) contains various menus from which you can select commands. Each Windows program that you run has a set of pull-down menus; Windows itself has a set too.

To open a menu, click on its name on the menu bar. Once a menu is open, you can select a command from it by clicking on the desired command.

> **Shortcut Keys** Notice that in Figure A.3, some commands are followed by key names such as Enter (for the **O**pen command) or F8 (for the **C**opy command). These are called *Shortcut Keys*. You can use these keys to perform the commands without even opening the menu.

Dimmed options   Shortcut keys

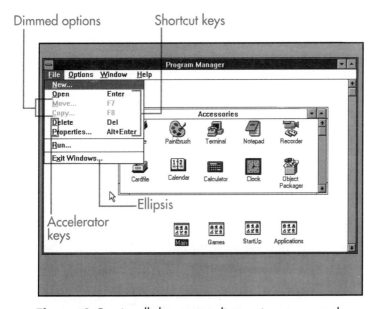

Figure A.3 A pull-down menu lists various commands you can perform.

Usually, when you select a command, the command is performed immediately. However:

- If the command name is gray (rather than black), the command is unavailable at the moment and you cannot choose it.

- If the command name is followed by an arrow, selecting the command will cause another menu to appear, from which you must select another command.

- If the command name is followed by an ellipsis (three dots), selecting it will cause a dialog box to appear. You'll learn about dialog boxes in the next section.

Navigating Dialog Boxes

A dialog box is Windows' way of requesting additional information. For example, if you choose **Print** from the **File** menu of the Write application, you'll see the dialog box shown in Figure A.4.

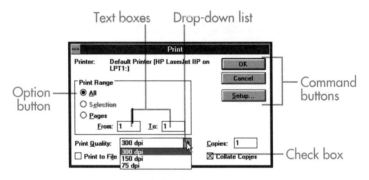

Figure A.4   A typical dialog box.

Each dialog box contains one or more of the following elements:

- *List boxes* display available choices. To activate a list, click inside the list box. If the entire list is not visible, use the scroll bar to view the items in the list. To select an item from the list, click on it.

- *Drop-down lists* are similar to list boxes, but only one item in the list is shown. To see the rest of the items, click on the down arrow to the right of the list box. To select an item from the list, click on it.

- *Text boxes* allow you to type an entry. To activate a text box, click inside it. To edit an existing entry, use the arrow keys to move the cursor and the Del or Backspace keys to delete existing characters, and then type your correction.

- *Check boxes* allow you to select one or more items in a group of options. For example, if you are styling text, you can select Bold and Italic to have the text appear in both bold and italic type. Click on a check box to activate it.

- *Option buttons* are like check boxes, but you can select only one option button in a group. Selecting one button unselects any option that is already selected. Click on an option button to activate it.

- *Command buttons* execute (or cancel) the command once you have made your selections in the dialog box. To press a command button, click on it.

Switching Between Windows

Many times you will have more than one window open at once. Some open windows may be program group windows, while others may be actual programs that are running. To switch among them, you can:

- Pull down the Window menu and choose the window you want to view

Or

- If a portion of the desired window is visible, click on it.

Controlling a Window

As you saw earlier in this appendix, you can minimize, maximize, and restore windows on your screen. But you can also move them and change their size.

- To move a window, drag its title bar to a different location. (Remember, drag means to hold down the left mouse button while you move the mouse.)

- To resize a window, position the mouse pointer on the border of the window until you see a double-headed arrow; then drag the window border to the desired size.

Copying Your Program Diskettes with File Manager

Before you install any new software, you should make a copy of the original diskettes as a safety precaution. Windows' File Manager makes this process easy.

First, start File Manager by double-clicking on the File Manager icon in the Main program group. Then, for each disk you need to copy, follow these steps:

1. Locate a blank disk of the same type as the original disk and label it to match the original. Make sure the disk you select does not contain any data that you want to keep.

2. Place the original disk in your diskette drive (A or B).

3. Open the Disk menu and select Copy Disk. The Copy Disk dialog box appears.

4. From the Source In list box, select the drive used in step 2.

5. Select the same drive from the Destination In list box. (Don't worry, File Manager will tell you to switch disks at the appropriate time.)

6. Select OK. The Confirm Copy Disk dialog box appears.

7. Select Yes to continue.

8. When you are instructed to insert the Source diskette, choose OK since you already did this in step 2. The Copying Disk box appears, and the copy process begins.

9. When you are instructed to insert the target disk, remove the original disk from the drive and insert the blank disk. Then choose OK to continue. The Copying Disk box disappears when the process is complete.

Index